W9-AOG-876

Council for
Exceptional
Children

The voice and vision of special education

Understanding IDEA 2004:
Frequently Asked Questions

ISBN 0-86586-432-2

Copyright © April 2007 by The Council for Exceptional Children,
1110 North Glebe Road, Suite 300, Arlington, Virginia 22201-5704.

Stock No. P5836

Printed in the United States of America.

10 9 8 7 6 5 4 3 2 1

Introduction

In 1975, Congress passed Public Law 94-142 (Education for All Handicapped Children Act), a law that gave new promises and new guarantees to children with disabilities. On December 3, 2004, President George W. Bush signed into law the Individuals With Disabilities Education Improvement Act of 2004, Public Law 108-446, often referred to as IDEA 2004. The United States Department of Education published the final regulations for Part B of the law on August 14, 2006. Because of the efforts of many over the past 32 years, IDEA has been an extremely effective law that has made significant progress in addressing the problems that existed when P.L. 94-142, was passed. IDEA 2004 demonstrates that Congress and the Administration is strongly committed to the right to a free appropriate public education (FAPE) for all children with disabilities. Close to 6.9 million children with disabilities are now receiving early intervention, special education, and related services under IDEA.

In its continuing efforts to inform and educate special educators and those who work on behalf of children and youth with disabilities, the Council for Exceptional Children has written *Understanding IDEA 2004 Frequently Asked Questions*, which answers the most relevant, frequently asked questions concerning IDEA 2004. This question-and-answer book on IDEA 2004 has been prepared to assist teachers, parents, researchers, higher education faculty, administrators, and related service providers in understanding what IDEA 2004 requires and how the provisions of the law and regulations impact services and programs for children with disabilities. These questions and answers are designed to provide the reader with a broad contextual framework for the significant changes that have been made in the law; it is not inclusive of every change or every topic covered by IDEA 2004. Accordingly, this publication is not intended to be a substitute for careful study and implementation of the IDEA 2004 regulations. *Understanding IDEA 2004 Frequently Asked Questions* includes language and provisions from the regulations that were issued for IDEA 2004 in August of 2006, and it supersedes the previous CEC question-and-answer publication that was written immediately after IDEA was signed into law but prior to the publication of the regulations. Regulations provide further interpretation of the law as needed, and regulations themselves have the force of law. This further interpretation of law is accomplished through regulatory definition, clarification, and qualification.

Please note that in writing *Understanding IDEA 2004 Frequently Asked Questions*, CEC has presented the IDEA topics in the order that they appear in both the law and the regulations, but each topic is addressed in separate chapters for ease of reference. Regulations for IDEA Part C and Part D had not been issued by the Department of Education at the time this publication went to print, although their statutory provisions are covered here. In addition, unless otherwise noted, any reference to "the regulations" or "regulatory language" means that the reference is to the IDEA 2004 regulations. Where we have drawn a comparison between specific language or provisions in the IDEA 1997 regulations and the IDEA 2004 regulations, the references to the different regulations will be explicitly spelled out.

Through IDEA reauthorization and other means, CEC continues to advocate for improved working conditions for all special educators and improved results for children and youth with disabilities and their families. Please check CEC's Policy and Advocacy Web site http://www.cec.sped.org/pp for more CEC resources on IDEA 2004 and the most up-to-date information on other policy issues that affect children with disabilities.

To read the IDEA 2004 law and regulations, please visit to CEC's Web site at http://www.cec.sped.org

Table of Contents

Miscellaneous

Appendix

Council for
Exceptional
Children
The voice and vision of special education

Understanding IDEA 2004:
Frequently Asked Questions

PART A
General Provisions

PART A General Provisions

FINDINGS

Q

What items were changed in the "Findings" section in Part A of the new IDEA 2004 law?

A

There were multiple changes to this section. In general, the various provisions were reordered, consolidated, and/or revised; new findings added; and data on minority children was updated. Additions to this section emphasized the following:

- Coordinating IDEA 2004 with improvement efforts under the Elementary and Secondary Education Act of 1965 (ESEA).

- Supporting intensive preservice preparation to improve the academic achievement and functional performance of children with disabilities, including the use of scientifically based instructional practices, to the maximum extent possible.

- Providing incentives for whole-school approaches, scientifically based early reading programs, positive behavioral interventions and supports, and early intervening services to reduce the need to label children as disabled in order to address the learning and behavioral needs of such children.

- Supporting the development and use of technology, including assistive technology devices and assistive technology services, to maximize accessibility for children with disabilities.

- Stating that, as the graduation rates for children with disabilities continue to climb, providing effective transition services to promote successful postschool employment or education as an important measure of accountability for children with disabilities.

DEFINITIONS

ASSISTIVE TECHNOLOGY DEVICE

Are surgically implanted medical devices – such as cochlear implants – considered an assistive technology device?

No, assistive technology devices do not include medical devices that are surgically implanted, or the replacement of such device, such as cochlear implants. However, schools are responsible for ensuring that the external aspect of any surgically implanted device is working properly. Therefore, schools must ensure that batteries are charged, the volume appropriate, etc.

CHARTER SCHOOL

Are charter schools considered public schools? What is the definition of a charter school?

Yes, charter schools are public schools that utilize nontraditional management systems and have greater flexibility while still adhering to state and local laws. Charter schools do not charge tuition and must remain nonsectarian in its programs, admission policies, employment practices, and other operations.

A definition of charter school was added to IDEA 2004, and it is identical to the one in Elementary and Secondary Education Act (ESEA) section 5210(1).

CHILD WITH A DISABILITY

There are many health conditions listed under the category "Other Health Impairment". Have there been any additions?

Yes, Tourette syndrome has been added to the list of chronic or acute health problems under the category Other Health Impairment, joining conditions such as asthma, attention deficit disorder, attention deficit/hyperactivity disorder, diabetes, epilepsy, a heart condition, to name a few.

Tourette syndrome was added to the list of Other Health Impairment to make it clear that Tourette syndrome is a neurological condition rather than a behavioral disorder.

Q *How does the new law address the definition of "child with a disability regarding a child ages 3 through 9"?*

A The new law adds language stating allowable subsets of age ranges for a child ages 3 through 9 who is experiencing a developmental delay. A child with a disability for children ages 3 through 9 now include the following language, "or any subset of that age range, including ages 3 though 5."

CORE ACADEMIC SUBJECTS

Q *What are the "core academic subjects" identified in the regulations?*

A The core academic subjects under IDEA 2004 are identical to those listed in the No Child Left Behind Act of 2001(NCLB): English, mathematics, civics and government science, reading or language arts, geography, economics, foreign languages, arts, and history.

ELEMENTARY SCHOOL

Q *How does the law define "elementary school"?*

A The law defines an elementary school as a nonprofit institutional day or residential school, including a public elementary charter school that provides elementary education under state law.

HIGHLY QUALIFIED SPECIAL EDUCATION TEACHERS

Q *What does "highly qualified" mean?*

A Congress included the term "highly qualified" in NCLB and IDEA 2004 to address the large numbers of general and special educators who were teaching subjects for which they were not prepared. In NCLB the term "highly qualified" focuses on ensuring that teachers are appropriately licensed and have an appropriate background in the "core academic subjects" they teach.

Q *If a special educator does not meet the requirements for being a highly qualified teacher, does that imply the teacher is not qualified?*

A No. All special educators must meet rigorous requirements to be licensed as a special educator. The federal law adds additional requirements focused on content knowledge to ensure that teachers have an appropriate content background in the core academic subjects they teach.

Q *How do highly qualified teacher requirements apply to special education teachers?*

A IDEA 2004 reflects the NCLB focus on ensuring that teachers are appropriately licensed and have an appropriate background in the core academic subjects they teach. IDEA 2004 requires that all special education teachers meet state certification/licensing requirements for being a special education teacher. In addition, when special educators directly teach core academic subjects, they must meet the highly qualified requirements for the respective core academic subjects.

Q *What are the requirements to be highly qualified for all special education teachers?*

A They must:

• Hold at least a Bachelor of Arts degree.

• Obtain full state special education certificates or equivalent licensure; and

• Cannot hold an emergency or temporary certificate.

Q *What are the requirements to be a highly qualified special education teacher for new or veteran elementary school teachers teaching one or more core academic subjects only to children with disabilities held to alternate academic standards?*

A In addition to the general requirements listed previously for all special education teachers, they may demonstrate academic subject competence through a high objective uniform state standard of evaluation (the HOUSSE process).

Q *What are the requirements to be a highly qualified special education teacher for a new or veteran middle or high school teacher teaching one or more core academic subjects only to children with disabilities held to alternate academic standards?*

A In addition to the general requirements listed previously for all special education teachers, they must demonstrate subject matter knowledge appropriate to the level of instruction being provided, as determined by the state to be needed to effectively teach to those standards.

Q *What are the requirements to be a highly qualified special education teacher for new teachers of two or more academic subjects who are highly qualified in mathematics, language arts, or science?*

A In addition to the general requirements listed previously for all special education teachers, he/she has a 2-year window in which to become highly qualified in the other core academic subjects and may do this through the HOUSSE process.

Q *What are the requirements to be a highly qualified special education teacher for veteran teachers who teach two or more core academic subjects only to children with disabilities?*

A In addition to the general requirements listed previously for all special education teachers, they may demonstrate academic subject competence through the HOUSSE process (including a single evaluation for all core academic subjects).

Q *What are the requirements to be a highly qualified special education teacher for consultative teachers and other special education teachers who do not teach core academic subjects?*

A They only need to meet the general requirements listed previously for all special education teachers.

Q *What are the requirements to be a highly qualified special education teacher for other special education teachers teaching core academic subjects?*

A In addition to the general requirements listed previously for all special education teachers, they must meet relevant ESEA requirements for new elementary school teachers, new middle/high schoolteachers, or veteran teachers.

Q *Can a special education teacher become highly qualified through alternative routes to certification?*

A Teachers are considered to meet the requirements for all special education teachers if they are participating in an alternative route to special education certification under which:

- They receive preservice and ongoing high quality professional development, have intensive supervision, teach for not more than

3 years under the alternative certification, demonstrate satisfactory progress toward full certification; and

• The state ensures, through its licensure or certification process, that teachers meet these requirements.

Q

A

What does the Congressional Report say about consultative teaching?

The House-Senate Conference Committee clarifies that, "for the purposes of the Elementary and Secondary Education Act of 1965 and the Individuals With Disabilities Education Act, a special education teacher who provides only consultative services to a highly qualified teacher (NCLB) should be considered a highly qualified special education teacher. Such consultative services do not include instruction in core academic subjects, but may include adjustments to the learning environment, modifications of instructional methods, adaptation of curricula, the use of positive behavioral supports and interventions, or the use of appropriate accommodations to meet the needs of individual children."

Q

A

What are the components of HOUSSE?

The high objective uniform state standard of evaluation, or HOUSSE, is a key component to the definition of a highly qualified teacher. It is a system through which existing teachers can demonstrate knowledge of their subject area without necessarily having to undertake further training or take a test. States have been given the latitude to create a HOUSSE that is unique to their licensure standards and teaching situations, thereby offering flexibility. Although there is no completely uniform definition for the types of HOUSSE systems being developed, there are several general categories evolving, including: a point system, professional development, performance evaluation, portfolio, and student achievement data.

Q

A

What are the components of a separate HOUSSE for special education teachers?

States may develop a separate HOUSSE for special education teachers:

• Provided it does not establish a lower standard for content knowledge than the general education HOUSSE; and

• Which may be a single HOUSSE evaluation covering multiple subjects.

Q

Do highly qualified teacher requirements apply to special education teachers who are teaching multiple subjects?

A

Yes. Special education teachers must meet highly qualified requirements in every core academic subject they teach to their students. These requirements apply whether special education teachers provide core academic instruction in a general education classroom, a resource room, or another setting.

Q

What activities may special education teachers carry out if they are not highly qualified in the core academic content areas being taught?

A

Special educators who do not meet the highly qualified requirements for core academic subjects may provide consultation to highly qualified teachers to help them individualize the curriculum through the use of behavioral supports and interventions or in the selection of appropriate accommodations in both learning and performance.

In addition, they may provide students with disabilities with content enrichment, reinforcement, and generalization, and assist students with learning and applying learning strategies such as study or organizational skills.

Q

Would the teacher who provides core academic instruction to students with disabilities need to be highly qualified in the core academic subject, even if the child already receives instruction in the same subject from a teacher who is highly qualified?

A

Yes. A special education teacher who provides instruction in core academic subjects needs to meet the requirements, even if he or she is not the only one instructing the students in that subject. However, if the special education teacher is reinforcing instruction or generalizing or maintaining learning, or is consulting with a teacher to help them individualize the instruction, the highly qualified teacher requirements do not apply.

Q

Do special education teachers in private schools need to meet the highly qualified teacher provisions in IDEA 2004?

A

The highly qualified teacher provisions do not apply to private school teachers, including those hired or contracted by a local education agency (LEA) to teach parentally placed private school children with disabilities.

How does the definition of the rule of construction apply to highly qualified teachers?

This definition does not create a right of action by a single student or class of students for failure of the teacher to be highly qualified. However, parents may file state complaints regarding staff qualifications.

What is the applicability of definition to ESEA and clarification of "new" special education teachers?

The applicability of definition to ESEA and clarification of "new" special education teachers are as follows:

- A teacher who is highly qualified under IDEA shall be considered highly qualified for purposes of the ESEA.

- A fully certified general education teacher who subsequently becomes fully certified or licensed as a special education teacher is a new special education teacher when first hired as a special education teacher.

HOMELESS CHILDREN

How is the term "homeless children" defined?

The new law adds the following definition: "The term homeless children has the meaning given the term homeless children and youths in section 725 of the McKinney-Vento Homeless Assistance Act (42 U.S.C.1143a)."

The definition of homeless children under the McKinney-Vento Homeless Assistance Act is:

"The term homeless children and youths - means individuals who lack a fixed, regular, and adequate nighttime residence; and includes:

- Children and youths who are sharing the housing of other persons due to loss of housing, economic hardship, or a similar reason; are living in motels, hotels, trailer parks, or camping grounds due to the lack of alternative adequate accommodations; are living in emergency or transitional shelters; are abandoned in hospitals; or are awaiting foster care placement;

- Children and youths who have a primary nighttime residence that is a public or private place not designed for or ordinarily used as a regular sleeping accommodation for human beings;

- Children and youths who are living in cars, parks, public spaces, abandoned buildings, substandard housing, bus or train stations, or similar settings; and

- Migratory children (as such term is defined in section 1309 of the Elementary and Secondary Education Act of 1965) who qualify as homeless for the purposes of this subtitle."

INFANT OR TODDLER WITH A DISABILITY

How does the new law address children with disabilities under 3 years of age?

The new law defines an infant or a toddler with a disability as being an individual under 3 years of age who needs early intervention services because the individual:

- Is experiencing developmental delays, as measured by appropriate diagnostic instruments and procedures in one or more of the areas of cognitive development, physical development, communication development, social or emotional development, and adaptive development; or

- Has a diagnosed physical or mental condition that has a high probability of resulting in a developmental delay; and

May also include at a state's discretion

- At-risk infants and toddlers; and

- Children with disabilities who are eligible for services under section 619 (addresses children 3-5 years of age) and who previously received services under Part C (addresses children birth-2 years of age) of IDEA 2004 until such children enter, or are eligible under state law to enter, kindergarten or elementary school, as appropriate, provided that any programs under Part C of the Act serving such children shall include:

  - An educational component that promotes school readiness and incorporates preliteracy, language, and numeracy skills; and

  - A written notification to parents of their rights and responsibilities in determining whether their child will continue to receive services under Part C of the Act or participate in preschool programs under section 619.

LIMITED ENGLISH PROFICIENT

Q

Does the definition of "limited English proficient" differ from what is in the ESEA?

A

No, the definition of limited English proficient in IDEA 2004 is identical to the definition that appears in the Elementary and Secondary Education act of 1965 and means a person who:

- Is 3 to 21 years old;

- Is enrolled or who is preparing to enroll in an elementary school or secondary school;

- Was not born in the United States or whose native language is a language other than English;

- Is a Native American or Alaska Native, or a native resident of the outlying areas; and who comes from an environment where a language other than English has had a significant impact on the individual's level of English language proficiency; or

- Is migratory, whose native language is a language other than English, and who comes from an environment where a language other than English is dominant; and

- Has difficulties in speaking, reading, writing, or understanding the English language that may be sufficient to deny the person: (a) the ability to meet the state's proficient level of achievement on state assessments described in section; (b) the ability to successfully achieve in classrooms where the language of instruction is English; or (c) the opportunity to participate fully in society.

PARENT

Q

How was the definition of "parent" expanded?

A

The definition of parent was expanded to include an adoptive parent, a foster parent (unless prohibited by state law), a guardian (unless the child is a ward of the state), or an individual legally responsible for the child. If there is more than one party that qualifies as a parent the biological or adoptive parent is assumed to be the parent except in cases where the biological or adoptive parent does not have legal authority. If a judicial decree or order identified a specific person to act as the parent of a child or to make educational decisions on behalf of a child, then such person shall be determined to be the parent for these purposes. In addition, the term "natural" parent was replaced with "biological" parent.

RELATED SERVICES

Q

What new services are included under the "related services" definition in the regulations?

A

The definition of related services has been expanded to now include interpreting services and school nurse services.

Interpreting services include:

- Oral transliteration services;

- Cued language services;

- Sign language transliteration services and interpreting services; and

- Transcription services (communication real-time translation [CART], C-Print, TypeWell)

Q

How has "related services" clarified surgically implanted devices?

A

The regulations now indicate that surgically implanted devices, including cochlear implants are not considered a related service. Related services do not include a medical device that is surgically implanted, the optimization of that device's functioning (e.g., mapping), maintenance of that device, or the replacement of that device. However, schools are responsible for ensuring that the external aspect of any surgically implanted device is working properly. Therefore, schools must ensure that batteries are charged, the volume appropriate, etc.

SCIENTIFICALLY BASED RESEARCH

Q

What is the definition of "scientifically based research?"

A

The term "scientifically based research" is woven throughout the law in various areas including when referencing instruction of children, identification of students with disabilities, and improvement of educational instruction under monitoring provisions, among other sections.

As defined in ESEA section 9101(37), scientifically based research:

- Means research that involves the application of rigorous, systematic, and objective procedures to obtain reliable and valid knowledge relevant to education activities and programs; and

- Includes research that--

  - Employs systematic, empirical methods that draw on observation or experiment;

– Involves rigorous data analyses that are adequate to test the stated hypotheses and justify the general conclusions drawn;

– Relies on measurements or observational methods that provide reliable and valid data across evaluators and observers, across multiple measurements and observations, and across studies by the same or different investigators;

– Is evaluated using experimental or quasi-experimental designs in which individuals, entities, programs, or activities are assigned to different conditions and with appropriate controls to evaluate the effects of the condition of interest, with a preference for random-assignment experiments, or other designs to the extent that those designs contain within-condition or across-condition controls;

– Ensures that experimental studies are presented in sufficient detail and clarity to allow for replication or, at a minimum, offer the opportunity to build systematically on their findings; and

– Has been accepted by a peer-reviewed journal or approved by a panel of independent experts through a comparably rigorous, objective, and scientific review.

SECONDARY SCHOOL

Q

What was added to the definition of "secondary school"?

A

The definition of "secondary school" now includes a public charter school.

SERVICES PLAN

Q

What is a "services plan" for parentally placed private school students with disabilities?

A

Services plan means a written statement that describes the special education and related services the LEA will provide to a parentally placed child with a disability who is enrolled in a private school and who has been designated to receive services, including the location of the services and any transportation necessary and is consistent with the other requirements detailed in the private school section of the regulations.

Q

SUPPLEMENTARY AIDS AND SERVICES

Are supplementary aids and services now expected to be provided in extracurricular and nonacademic settings?

A

Yes. The definition of "supplementary aids and services" has been expanded to now state that aids, services, and other supports are provided in general education classes, other education related settings, and in extracurricular and nonacademic settings. The inclusion of extracurricular and nonacademic settings was added to enable that students with disabilities are educated with their nondisabled peers to the maximum extent appropriate.

TRANSITION SERVICES

Q

Are "transition services" changed under the new law?

A

The term "transition services" means a coordinated set of activities for a child with a disability that:

- Is designed to be within a results-oriented process that is focused on improving the academic and functional achievement of the child with a disability to facilitate the child's movement from school to postschool activities, including postsecondary education, vocational education, integrated employment (including supported employment), continuing and adult education, adult services, independent living, or community participation;

- Is based on the individual child's needs, taking into account the child's strengths, preferences, and interests; and

- Includes instruction, related services, community experiences, the development of employment and other postschool adult living objectives, and, when appropriate, acquisition of daily living skills and functional vocational evaluation.

UNIVERSAL DESIGN

Q

How is "universal design" defined?

A

The term "universal design" means a concept or philosophy for designing and delivering products and services that are usable by people with the widest possible range of functional capabilities, which include products and services that are directly accessible (without requiring assistive technologies) and products and services that are interoperable with assistive technologies. This term has the meaning given in the Assistive Technology Act of 1998.

Q

A

WARD OF THE STATE

Does the definition of "ward of the state" include foster children and children in the custody of a public child welfare agency?

Yes, a "ward of the state" includes foster children and children in the custody of a public child welfare agency, as defined by the state. However, it does not include a foster child who has a foster parent who meets the definition of parent.

Council for
Exceptional
Children
The voice and vision of special education

Understanding IDEA 2004:
Frequently Asked Questions

PART B
Assistance for Education of
All Children With Disabilities

PART B Assistance for Education of All Children With Disabilities

LEAST RESTRICTIVE ENVIRONMENT

Q

What changes concerning state funding mechanisms were made to least restrictive environment (LRE)?

A

Least restrictive environment provisions were modified and enhanced as follows:

- A state shall not use a funding mechanism by which the state distributes funds on the basis of the type of setting in which a child is served that will result in the failure to provide a child with a disability a free appropriate public education (FAPE) according to the unique needs of the child as described in the child's individualized education program (IEP).

- The following language was included in the conference report to clarify the language in the law: "The conferees are concerned that some States continue to use funding mechanisms that provide financial incentives for, and disincentives against, certain placements. It is the intent of the changes to prevent State funding mechanisms from affecting appropriate placement decisions for students with disabilities."

Q

What changes have been made regarding LRE in academic and nonacademic settings?

A

The public agency must ensure that each child with a disability participates with nondisabled children in the extracurricular services and activities to the maximum extent appropriate to the needs of that child. Due to IDEA 2004, the public agency must also ensure that each child with a disability has the supplementary aids and services determined by the child's IEP Team to be appropriate and necessary for the child to participate in nonacademic settings.

CHILDREN IN PRIVATE SCHOOLS

CHILDREN WITH DISABILITIES ENROLLED BY THEIR PARENTS IN PRIVATE SCHOOLS

Q

What is the definition of "parentally placed private school children with disabilities"?

A

According to the regulations, "parentally placed private school children with disabilities" means children with disabilities enrolled by their parents in private, including religious, schools or facilities that meet the definition of elementary school or secondary school, as determined by state law, other than children with disabilities who are placed by public agencies.

Q

Under the regulations, who is responsible for child find, including the cost of individual evaluations, and services for parentally placed children in private schools?

A

In IDEA 2004, the LEA where the private school is located, not the LEA of the child's residence, is now responsible for child find and the provision of services for parentally placed private school children with disabilities. This is a change from IDEA 1997 under which the LEA of the child's residence was responsible for child find and services.

In addition, the activities undertaken to carry out this responsibility for private school children with disabilities must be similar to activities undertaken for children with disabilities in public schools.

Each LEA where the private school is located, must locate, identify, and evaluate all children with disabilities who are enrolled by their parents in private school, as part of the child find process.

The cost of carrying out child find includes the cost of individual evaluations.

Q

Are LEAs responsible for child find for out-of-state parentally placed private school children?

A

Yes. This new provision applies to out-of-state parentally placed private school children as well. In its discussion of the regulations, the Department of Education states that the law is clear that the LEA where the private school is located is responsible for child find and that the law does not provide an exception for children who reside in one state and attend private schools in other states.

Q

A

Does the provision of special education and services to a parentally placed private school child entitle the child to FAPE?

No. In its discussion of the regulations, the Department of Education stated, "The definition of services plan was included to describe the content, development, and implementation of plans for parentally placed private school children with disabilities who have been designated to receive equitable services. The definition cross references the specific requirements for the provision of services to parentally placed private school children with disabilities, which provide that parentally placed private school children have no individual right to special education and related services thus are not entitled to FAPE."

The IDEA 2004 regulations did not make any changes to the provisions of FAPE from the 1997 regulations.

Q

What is included in a services plan for parentally placed private school children with disabilities?

A services plan must be developed and implemented for each private school child with a disability who has been designated by the LEA, where the private school is located, to receive special education and related services. The LEA must make the final decisions with respect to the services to be provided to eligible parentally placed private school children with disabilities.

Q

What records must an LEA maintain on parentally placed private school children?

Each LEA must maintain in its records the following information related to parentally placed private school children:

• The number of children evaluated;

• The number of children determined to be children with disabilities; and

• The number of children served.

The LEA must provide this information to the SEA as well.

Q

A

How are IDEA 2004 Part B funds to be spent on parentally placed children in private schools?

LEAs must spend a proportionate share of Part B and preschool funds for parentally placed private school children with disabilities in the LEA's jurisdiction.

For example, let's say an LEA has 340 eligible public school children with disabilities, and there are 45 parentally placed private school children in the LEA. Let's also say that the total federal flow through of IDEA 2004 funds for that LEA is $176,500. To find the proportionate share of funds to be spent on the parentally placed private school children, take the total federal flow through ($176,500) and divide it by number of eligible children with disabilities (385) in the LEA. That comes to $458.44 per child. Multiply this figure by the number of parentally placed children in private schools (45), and you come up with the proportionate share that the LEA must spend on the parentally placed private school children. In this case, 45 x $458.44 = $20,630. That total is the proportionate share that must be spent on parentally placed private school children in the LEA.

The cost of carrying out child find requirements, including individual evaluations, may not be considered.

Q

Must an LEA carry its unspent IDEA 2004 Part B and 619 proportionate share of funds over into the next year?

A

Yes. This proportionate share of funds must be spent or carried over into the following year. If an LEA has not spent all of its equitable services funds by the end of the fiscal year, the LEA must obligate the remaining funds for special education and related services, including direct services, to parentally placed private school children with disabilities for an additional one-year carry-over period year.

This is a new requirement in the regulations.

Q

How do the private school and the LEA where it is located consult on services for parentally placed children in private schools?

A

The LEA must consult with private school officials and the parents of parentally placed private school children with disabilities in the following five areas:

- The child find process, including how parentally placed private school children suspected of having a disability can participate equitably and how parents, teachers, and private school officials will be informed of the process.

- The determination of the proportionate share of funds available to serve parentally placed private school children with disabilities, including the determination of how the proportionate share of those funds was calculated.

- The consultation process among the LEA, private school officials, and representatives of parents of parentally placed private school children with disabilities, including how the process will operate throughout the school year to ensure that parentally placed children with disabilities identified through the child find process can meaningfully participate in special education and related services.

- How, where, and by whom special education and related services will be provided for parentally placed private school children with disabilities, including a discussion of:

  - The types of services, including direct services and alternate service delivery mechanisms;

  - How special education and related services will be apportioned if funds are insufficient to serve all parentally placed private school children; and

  - How and when those decisions will be made.

- How, if the LEA disagrees with the views of the private school officials on the provision of services or the types of services, whether provided directly or through a contract, the LEA will provide to the private school officials a written explanation of the reasons why the LEA chose not to provide services directly or through a contract.

Q

What must an LEA do to document that consultation with the private school representatives was timely and meaningful?

A

When timely and meaningful consultation has occurred, the LEA must obtain a written affirmation signed by the representatives of participating private schools. If the representatives do not provide the affirmation within a reasonable period of time, the LEA must forward the documentation of the consultation process to the SEA.

This is a new provision in the regulations.

Q

Can a private school official file complaints against the LEA if they believe the LEA did not meet the consultation requirements?

A

A private school may file a complaint with the SEA that the LEA did not consult with the private school in a timely and meaningful manner or that the LEA did not consider the private school officials' views.

If the private school official wishes to submit a complaint, the official must provide to the SEA the basis of the noncompliance by the LEA with the applicable private school provisions, and the LEA must forward the appropriate documentation to the SEA.

If dissatisfied with the SEA ruling on the complaint against the LEA, the private school may then file the complaint with the U.S. Secretary of Education, in which case the SEA must forward all complaint documentation to the Secretary.

Can a parent who has placed his or her child in a private school file a due process complaint against the LEA?

A parent may only file a due process complaint based on child find requirements. No parentally placed private school child with a disability has an individual right to receive some or all of the special education and related services that the child would receive if enrolled in a public school.

The Department of Education states, "Child find...is a part of the basic obligation that public agencies have to all children with disabilities, and failure to locate, identify, and evaluate a parentally placed private school child would be subject to due process. Therefore, the due process provisions...do apply to complaints that the LEA where the private school is located failed to meet the consent and evaluation requirements" for parentally placed private school children.

A new provision in the regulations states that any due process complaint regarding child find requirements must be filed with the LEA in which the private school is located and a copy must be forwarded to the SEA.

Under what conditions can a parent file a complaint against a state for failing to comply with the provisions regarding parentally placed private school children?

Any complaint that an SEA or LEA has failed to meet the requirements for parentally placed private school children must be filed according to the procedures described in the state complaint procedures.

Do private school teachers who provide services to children with disabilities enrolled in private schools have to meet the highly qualified teacher provisions of IDEA 2004?

No. Private school teachers are not required to meet the requirements of Highly Qualified Teachers under IDEA 2004 and NCLB.

What personnel must provide equitable services?

Provision of equitable services must be provided by employees of a public agency, or through contract by the public agency with an individual, association, agency, organization, or other entity.

In addition, special education and related services provided to parentally placed private school children with disabilities, including materials and equipment, must be secular, neutral, and nonideological.

Q

Can the LEA where the child resides and a private school outside of that LEA share information about a child who is about to enroll in the private school by his or her parents?

A

Yes, but only if the parents of the child consent beforehand. If a child is enrolled in, or is going to enroll in, a private school in an LEA outside of the child's residence, parental consent must be obtained before personally identifiable information about the child is shared between the LEA where the private school is located and the LEA where the child's parents reside.

CHILDREN WITH DISABILITIES IN PRIVATE SCHOOLS PLACED OR REFERRED BY PUBLIC AGENCIES

Q

Did the regulations change any aspect of the state's responsibility to provide FAPE to a child with a disability placed or referred by a public agency?

A

Yes. As in the IDEA 1997 regulations, FAPE provisions apply only to children with disabilities who are or have been placed in or referred to a private school or facility by a public agency as a means of providing special education and related services. However, under the IDEA 2004 regulations, highly qualified teacher and personnel qualifications provisions do not apply in these circumstances. In its discussion of the regulations, the U.S. Department of Education states, "When the public agency chooses to place a child with a significant disability, or any child with a disability, in a private school as a means of providing FAPE, the public agency has an obligation to ensure that the child receives FAPE to the same extent the child would if placed in a public school, irrespective of whether the private school teachers meet the highly qualified teacher requirements."

CHILDREN WITH DISABILITIES ENROLLED BY THEIR PARENTS IN PRIVATE SCHOOLS WHEN FAPE IS AT ISSUE

Q

Were there any significant changes made to the provisions regarding the placement of children in private schools by their parents when FAPE is at issue?

A

No. The regulations did not make significant changes to these provisions.

STATE COMPLAINT PROCEDURES

Can private school officials file a complaint against the LEA if they believe the LEA did not meet the consultation requirements regarding parentally placed children with disabilities?

A private school may file a complaint with the SEA that the LEA did not consult with the private school in a timely and meaningful manner or that the LEA did not consider the private school officials' views.

If the private school official wishes to submit a complaint, the official must provide to the SEA the basis of the noncompliance by the LEA with the applicable private school provisions, and the LEA must forward the appropriate documentation to the SEA.

If dissatisfied with the SEA ruling on the complaint against the LEA, the private school official may then file the complaint with the U.S. Secretary of Education, in which case the SEA must forward all appropriate complaint documentation to the Secretary.

This is a new provision in the regulations that only applies to parentally placed private school children with disabilities.

Are there any new provisions under the time limit provisions for state complaint procedures?

Yes. Although most of the IDEA 2004 regulations time limit provisions are consistent with the IDEA 1997 regulations, there are two new provisions under the 60-day time limit. These new provisions provide the public agency with the opportunity to respond to the complaint within 60 days, and must include, at a minimum:

- At the discretion of the public agency, a proposal to resolve the complaint; and

- An opportunity for a parent who has filed a complaint and the public agency to voluntarily engage in mediation consistent with the mediation requirements under the procedural safeguards provisions in IDEA 2004.

Can the 60-day time limit be extended for parents and LEAs if they are engaged in mediation?

Yes. Under the regulations, a new provision was added that says a state must allow an extension of time only if parents, or other individuals or organizations, and the LEA involved agree to extend the time to engage in mediation or to engage in other alternative means of dispute resolution if an alternative means is available in the state.

Q

Is there any new information that is required for complaints under the regulations?

A

In addition to the information that was previously required under the IDEA 1997 regulations, the IDEA 2004 regulations require that the following new requirements be included in a complaint:

- The signature and contact information for the complainant; and

- If the complaint alleges violations with respect to a specific child—

  - The name and address of the residence of the child;

  - The name of the school the child is attending;

  - In the case of a homeless child or youth, available contact information for the child and the name of the school the child is attending;

  - A description of the nature of the problem of the child, including facts relating to the problem; and

  - A proposed resolution of the problem to the extent known and available to the party at the time the complaint is filed.

- Further, a complaint must allege a violation that occurred not more than 1 year prior to the date that the complaint is received.

Language from the IDEA 2004 regulations is identical to language from the IDEA 1997 regulations, except the IDEA 2004 regulations delete language from the IDEA 1997 language that states "unless a longer period is reasonable because the violation is continuing, or the complainant is requesting compensatory services for a violation that occurred not more than three years prior to the date the complaint is received."

The U.S. Department of Education, in its discussion of the IDEA 2004 regulations, states that, "We believe a one-year timeline is reasonable and will assist in smooth implementation of the State complaint procedures. The references to longer periods for continuing violations and for compensatory services claims in current [regulations] were removed to ensure expedited resolution for public agencies and children with disabilities. Limiting a complaint to a violation that occurred not more than one year prior to the date that the complaint is received will help ensure that problems are raised and addressed promptly so that children receive FAPE. We believe longer time limits are not generally effective and beneficial to the child because the issues in a State complaint become so stale that they are unlikely to be resolved. However, States may choose to accept and resolve complaints regarding alleged violations that occurred outside the one-year timeline, just as they are free to add additional protections in other areas that are not inconsistent with the requirements of the Act and its implementing regulations. For these reasons, we do not believe it is necessary to retain the language."

• Finally, the complainant must forward a copy of the complaint to the LEA or public agency serving the child at the same time the complainant files the complaint with the SEA.

In its discussion of the regulations, the Department of Education said that "The purpose of requiring the party filing the complaint to forward a copy of the complaint to the LEA or public agency serving the child, at the same time the party files the complaint with the SEA, is to ensure that the public agency involved has knowledge of the issues and an opportunity to resolve them directly with the complaining party at the earliest possible time. The sooner the LEA knows that a complaint is filed and the nature of the issue(s), the quicker the LEA can work directly with the complainant to resolve the complaint. We believe the benefit of having the complainant forward a copy of the complaint to the LEA or public agency far outweigh the minimal burden placed on the complainant because it will lead to a faster resolution of the complaint at the local level. For these reasons, we also do not believe it is more efficient to have the SEA forward the complaint to the public agency or provide the public agency with a statement summarizing the complaint."

PERSONNEL QUALIFICATIONS

What changes were made to the provisions regarding personnel qualifications?

Multiple changes were made as follows:

• Deleted the comprehensive system of personnel development (CSPD) requirement.

• Changed the term "standards" to "qualifications."

• Added the language to requirements that personnel have content knowledge and skills to serve children with disabilities.

• Deleted the "highest standards" language and the language on good faith efforts and shortage of personnel.

• Added language related to qualifications of special education teachers at the elementary, middle, or secondary level without mentioning preschool teachers.

• Added language regarding qualifications of related services personnel and paraprofessionals.

• Added a construction clause stating that notwithstanding any other individual right of action that a parent or student may maintain, nothing in this section shall be construed to create a right of action on behalf of an individual student for the failure of a particular state educational agency or local educational agency staff person to be highly qualified, or to prevent a parent from filing a complaint about staff qualifications with the state educational agency.

Q

What change was made to the provision regarding qualifications of related services personnel and paraprofessionals?

A

A provision was added that states that related services personnel and paraprofessionals who deliver services in their discipline or profession meet the requirements regarding SEA qualifications and have not had certification or licensure requirements waived on an emergency, temporary, or provisional basis.

Congressional IDEA 2004 Report language regarding this provision states that Conferees are cognizant of the difficulties that some LEAs have experienced in recruiting and retaining qualified related services providers and have provided greater flexibility to SEAs to establish appropriate personnel standards.

Conferees are concerned that language in current law regarding the qualifications of related services providers has established an unreasonable standard for SEAs to meet, and as a result, has led to a shortage of the availability of related services for students with disabilities.

Conferees intend for SEAs to establish rigorous qualifications for related services providers to ensure that students with disabilities receive the appropriate quality and quantity of care. SEAs are encouraged to consult with LEAs, other state agencies, the disability community, and professional organizations to determine the appropriate qualifications for related service providers, including the use of consultative, supervisory, and collaborative models to ensure that students with disabilities receive the services described in their individual IEPs.

Q

Can paraprofessionals and assistants assist in the provision of special education and related services?

A

Paraprofessionals and assistants who are appropriately trained and supervised may assist in the provision of special education and related services.

Q

When do special education teachers need to be highly qualified?

A

Public school special education teachers must be highly qualified by the deadline established in No Child Left Behind.

Q

IDEA 2004 refers to "measurable steps" requirements. What are SEAs and LEAs required to do?

A

A state must adapt a policy that requires LEAs to take "measurable steps" to recruit, hire, train, and retain highly qualified personnel to provide special education and related services.

Q

Does the LEA have responsibilities for personnel development?

A

Yes, the LEA must ensure that all personnel necessary who deliver special education and related services are appropriately and adequately prepared.

STATE ADMINISTRATION

Q

What are the new provisions for state administration regarding the development of state rules, regulations, and policies?

A

IDEA 2004 adds the following provisions:

- Each state that receives funds under this title must:

  - Ensure that any state rules, regulations, and policies relating to this title conform to the purposes of IDEA Part B;

  - Identify in writing to LEAs located in the state and the Secretary of Education any such rule, regulation, or policy as a state-imposed requirement that is not required by Part B and federal regulations; and

  - Minimize the number of rules, regulations, and policies to which the LEAs and schools located in the state are subject under Part B this title.

- State rules, regulations, and policies under Part B must support and facilitate LEA and school-level system improvement designed to enable children with disabilities to meet the challenging state student academic achievement standards.

Q

A

Are there any provisions in the new law for paperwork reduction?

Yes. The following new section was added:

- The establishment of a pilot program so that up to 15 states may receive authority from the Secretary of the Department of Education to waive Part B requirements for no more than 4 years to reduce paperwork and noninstructional time burdens that do not assist in improving educational and functional results.

- The requirement that civil rights cannot be waived and nothing can affect the right to FAPE or waive procedural safeguards.

- Submission of a proposal by a state that wants to participate in the paperwork reduction pilot program, including listing requirements that would be waived.

- Termination of the waiver if the state needs assistance or intervention as a result of federal oversight or if the state fails to implement the waiver appropriately.

- Reporting to Congress by the Secretary on the effectiveness of the waivers and recommendations for broader implementation.

PERFORMANCE GOALS AND INDICATORS

Q

A

What significant changes were made to provisions around performance goals and indicators under the regulations?

Under the regulations, a state must have in effect established goals for the performance of children with disabilities that include several new or revised provisions:

- The goals must be the same as the state's objectives for progress by children in its definition of adequate yearly progress (AYP), including the state's objectives for progress by children with disabilities under the ESEA; and

- The goals must address graduation rates and dropout rates, as well as other factors as the State may determine.

The provision for goals that promote the purposes of IDEA 2004 Part B and the provision that the goals be "consistent, to the extent appropriate, with any other goals and academic standards for children established by the state" is consistent with the IDEA 1997 regulations. However, the IDEA 2004 statute and regulations remove the word "maximum" before "extent appropriate" and remove the word "all" before "children" from the IDEA 1997 regulations.

Q *What indicators must a state have for assessing the progress towards meeting the performance goals?*

A States must have in effect established performance indicators to assess progress toward achieving the goals described previously. Those indicators must also include measurable annual objectives for progress by children with disabilities under NCLB.

Q *How are states required to report on the progress toward meeting their annual goals?*

A States are now required to report annually to the Secretary of the Department of Education and the public on the progress of the state, and the progress of children with disabilities toward meeting the goals outlined in the first question and must include any reporting requirements under NCLB.

ACCESS TO INSTRUCTIONAL MATERIALS

Q *What is National Instructional Materials Accessibility Standard?*

A According to the regulations, the term "National Instructional Materials Accessibility Standard" (NIMAS) means the standard established by the Secretary of the Department of Education to be used in the preparation of electronic files suitable and used solely for efficient conversion into specialized formats.

NIMAS regulations were first published in the Federal Register on July 19, 2006 and were included as an appendix in the final IDEA 2004 regulations when they were published in the Federal Register on August 14, 2006.

Q *For whom is NIMAS intended?*

A NIMAS is intended for blind persons or other persons with print disabilities. This means children served under IDEA 2004 Part B who may qualify to receive books and other publications produced in specialized formats consistent with the law entitled An Act to Provide Books for the Adult Blind, which was enacted in 1931.

Library of Congress regulations related to the Act to Provide Books for the Adult Blind provides that blind persons or persons with print disabilities include:

• Blind persons whose visual acuity, as determined by competent authority, is 20/200 or less in the better eye with correcting glasses, or whose widest diameter if visual field subtends an angular distance no greater than 20 degrees.

- Persons whose visual disability, with correction and regardless of optical measurement, is certified by competent authority as preventing the reading of standard printed material.

- Persons certified by competent authority as unable to read or unable to use standard printed material as a result of physical limitations.

- Persons certified by competent authority as having a reading disability resulting from organic dysfunction and of sufficient severity to prevent their reading printed material in a normal manner.

Q

What is NIMAC and what is its role?

A

NIMAC is the National Instructional Materials Accessibility Center. The American Printing House for the Blind operates this Center, which is funded by the U.S. Department of Education

The role of NIMAC is:

- To receive and maintain a catalog of print instructional materials prepared in the NIMAS, as established by the Secretary, made available to such center by the textbook publishing industry, SEAs, and LEAs;

- To provide access to print instructional materials, including textbooks, in accessible media, free of charge, to blind or other persons with print disabilities in elementary schools and secondary schools; and

- To develop, adopt, and publish procedures to protect against copyright infringement with respect to the print instructional materials provisions.

Q

What are print instructional materials?

A

Print instructional materials are defined as printed textbooks and related printed core materials that are written and published primarily for use in elementary school and secondary school instruction and are required by an SEA or LEA for use by students in the classroom.

Responding to several comments as to whether NIMAS regulations are limited to print instructional materials, the Department of Education stated, "The NIMAS is the standard established by the Secretary to be used in the preparation of electronic files of print instructional materials so they can be more easily converted to accessible formats, such as Braille. In addition to print materials, the NIMAS provides standards for textbooks and related core materials where icons replace text. Materials with icons will be available if they are in printed textbooks and related printed core materials that are written and published primarily for use in elementary school and secondary school instruction and are required by an SEA or LEA for use by children in the classroom, consistent with...the Act."

Q *Are states required to adopt NIMAS?*

A Yes. All states are required to adopt NIMAS in a "timely manner." States must establish a definition of "timely manner." By the fall of 2006, all states had adopted NIMAS.

Q *Are states required to coordinate with NIMAC?*

A No. States are not required to coordinate with NIMAC. If a state chooses not to coordinate with NIMAC, it must assure the U.S. Secretary of Education that it will provide instructional materials to blind persons or other persons with print disabilities in a timely manner. In accomplishing that goal, the SEA must ensure that all public agencies take all reasonable steps to provide instructional materials in accessible formats to children with disabilities who need those instructional materials at the same time as other children receive instructional materials.

Q *If a state decides to coordinate with the NIMAC, what must it do?*

A If a state decides to coordinate with NIMAC, then by December 3, 2006, the state must have entered into a written contract with the publisher of the print instructional materials to:

• Require the publisher to provide to NIMAC electronic files containing the contents of the print instructional materials using the NIMAS on or before delivery of the print instructional materials; or

• The SEA must purchase instructional materials from the publisher that are produced in or rendered in specialized formats.

• The SEA must also provide instructional materials to blind persons or other persons with print disabilities in a timely manner.

• The state must also, to the maximum extent possible, coordinate with the state agency that administers assistive technology programs.

Every state has indicated that it will opt into the NIMAC.

Q
A

Are LEAs required to coordinate with the NIMAC?

No. LEAs are not required to coordinate with the NIMAC. If an LEA chooses not to coordinate with the NIMAC, it must provide assurance to the state that it will provide instructional materials to blind persons or persons with print disabilities in a timely manner.

However, nothing in the regulations relieves an LEA from its responsibility to ensure that children with disabilities who need print in accessible formats, but who are not included in the definition of a blind or other person with print disabilities under the regulations, or those who need materials that cannot be produced from NIMAS files, receive those materials in a timely manner.

If an LEA does elect to coordinate with NIMAC when purchasing print instructional materials, it must acquire the materials in the same manner and under the same conditions that an SEA must meet.

OVERIDENTIFICATION AND DISPROPORTIONALITY

Q
A

What provisions do the regulations include to address disproportionality?

According to the regulations, states must have in effect policies and procedures, consistent with the program information data reporting requirements of the law, designed to prevent the inappropriate overidentification or disproportionate representation by race and ethnicity of children as children with disabilities, including children with disabilities with a particular impairment. Each state is responsible for developing its own definition of "disproportionality" for use in that state.

Q
A

How are states to monitor disproportionate representation of racial and ethnic groups in special education?

Under the state monitoring and enforcement provisions of the regulations, states must monitor LEAs using quantifiable indicators in a number of areas, including the disproportionate representation of racial and ethnic groups in special education and related services. States are required to monitor the extent to which the representation is the result of inappropriate identification.

Q
A

Under what areas are states required to collect data to determine whether disproportionality is taking place in the LEAs?

Every state that receives funds under IDEA Part B, and the Secretary of the Interior, is required to provide for the collection and examination of data to determine if significant disproportionality based on race and ethnicity is occurring in the state and LEAs with respect to the following three areas:

- The identification of children as children with disabilities, including the identification of children as children with disabilities in accordance with a particular impairments defined in the regulations;

- The placement in particular educational settings of these children; and

- The incidence, duration, and type of disciplinary actions, including suspensions and expulsions.

Q
A

What steps must be taken if an LEA is found to have significant disproportionality?

According to the regulations, if an LEA is determined to have significant disproportionality with respect to the identification of children as children with disabilities, or the placement in particular educational settings of those children, the state, or the Secretary of the Interior must:

- Provide for the review and, if appropriate, revision of the policies, procedures, and practices used in the identification or placement to ensure that the policies, procedures, and practices comply with the requirements of the law;

- Require any LEA identified as having significant disproportionality to reserve the maximum funds (15%) for early intervening services to provide comprehensive coordinated early intervening services to serve children in the LEA, particularly, but not exclusively, children in those groups that were significantly overidentified; and

- Require the LEA to publicly report on its revision of policies, practices, and procedures used in the identification or placement of students.

PROHIBITION ON MANDATORY MEDICATION

Q

Can an SEA or LEA require a child to take medication as a requirement for attendance at school?

A

No.

- The SEA shall prohibit state and local educational agency personnel from requiring a child to obtain a prescription for a substance covered by the Controlled Substances Act as a condition of attending school, receiving an evaluation, or receiving special education services.

- This provision does not prohibit teachers and other school personnel from consulting or sharing classroom-based observations with parents or guardians regarding a student's academic and functional performance, or behavior in the classroom or school, or regarding the need for evaluation for special education or related services under child find.

PARTICIPATION IN ASSESSMENTS

[NOTE: The U.S. Department of Education had not issued final regulations for this section by the time this publication went to print in April of 2007. This section, which is currently marked "Reserved" in the IDEA 2004 Part B regulations, is for regulations regarding assessments for those students who are identified as requiring modified assessments based on modified achievement standards, or approximately 2% of students who need modified assessments, but who do not require alternate assessments based on alternate achievement standards.

The Department of Education released proposed regulations on this section on December 15, 2005. CEC will provide updates and analysis on the final regulations for this section when they are issued by the Department of Education. The question that follows is based upon language in IDEA 2004.]

Q

What changes were made to the provision on participation in assessments?

A

IDEA 2004 made multiple changes to this requirement, including:

- Added the word "all" before "children" and before "general State and district-wide assessment programs, including assessments described under section 1111 of the Elementary and Secondary Education Act of 1965" and added the phrase "requiring alternate assessments where necessary as indicated in their respective individualized education programs."

- Added a requirement that a state (or, in the case of a districtwide assessment, the LEA) develop and implement guidelines for the participation of children with disabilities in alternate assessments for those children who cannot participate in regular assessments, with accommodations as indicated in their respective IEPs.

- Added to the requirements for alternate assessments that the guidelines shall provide for alternate assessments that:

  - Are aligned with the state's challenging academic content standards and challenging student academic achievement standards; and

  - If the state has adopted alternate academic achievement standards permitted under the regulations promulgated to carry out section 1111(b)(1) of the Elementary and Secondary Education Act of 1965, measure the achievement of children with disabilities against those standards.

- Added the LEA to the requirements to publicly report on assessment results and added a requirement that the SEA and the LEA must also report on the number of children who were provided accommodations in order to participate in regular assessments.

- Added a new provision on universal design. The SEA (or, in the case of a districtwide assessment, the LEA) shall, to the extent feasible, use universal design principles in developing and administering any assessments under this paragraph.

EARLY INTERVENING SERVICES

Q

What are Early Intervening Services?

A

Early Intervening Services (EIS) are supports for children and educators to address the educational needs of children in the general education setting. EIS provides academic and behavioral supports for general education children who have not been identified as in need of special education, but have been recognized by the general education teacher as needing additional educational or behavioral supports to succeed in the classroom. In addition, EIS funds can be used for professional development to train staff on delivering scientifically based academic/behavioral interventions. EIS funds can also provide educational and behavioral evaluations, services and supports, including scientifically based literacy instruction.

Q
A

Who is eligible to receive EIS?

Children in kindergarten through Grade 12 (with an emphasis on kindergarten-Grade 3) who are not currently identified as needing special education or related services are eligible to receive EIS.

EIS cannot limit access to a FAPE nor does it create a right to FAPE. In addition, the delivery of EIS cannot delay the evaluation of a child suspected of having a disability.

Q
A

How may EIS be funded?

EIS may be funded jointly under IDEA and the Elementary and Secondary Education Act (ESEA, known as No Child Left Behind) and may use interagency funding structures. LEAs may use up to 15% of the Part B subgrant to fund EIS programs less any amount reduced by the LEA pursuant to adjustments to local fiscal efforts including excess cost and maintenance of effort in certain years. The LEA must use 15% of its Part B subgrant to fund EIS if it is shown to have disproportionality.

Q
A

What are the funding requirements if an LEA is found to have disproportionality based on race or ethnicity?

If an LEA has a significant disproportionate number of children with disabilities, children in particular education settings (including special education), or children who have been disciplined (suspended, expelled, etc.) based on race or ethnicity, then the state must require an LEA to use the full 15% of Part B funds to fund EIS, particularly, but not exclusively to those groups that were significantly overidentified. In addition, the state must require the LEA to review, revise if appropriate, and publicly report on the revision of policies, procedures, and practices used in the identification or placement to ensure that the policies, procedures, and practices comply with the IDEA 2004 requirements.

Q
A

What are the reporting requirements for EIS?

Annually, LEAs must report to the SEA the following during the preceding 2-year period:

• Number of children who receive EIS ; and

• Number of children who, after receiving EIS, went on to receive special education.

Q

Do Early Intervening Services create a right to a FAPE?

A

No. Because EIS are not considered special education, EIS does not create a right to FAPE. Similarly, EIS cannot limit FAPE and cannot delay the evaluation of a child suspected of having a disability.

PARENTAL CONSENT, EVALUATIONS, AND REEVALUATIONS

Q

Is there a practical difference in the use of the terms "consent," "informed consent," "parental consent," "agree," and "agreement" in the final Part B regulations?

A

Yes. The term "consent" is specifically defined in the Part B regulations. The definition requires that a parent be fully informed of all information relevant to the activity for which consent is being requested and that a parent agree in writing when giving consent. Consent must be both "informed" and "written." The terms "consent," "informed consent," "parental consent," and "written consent" are all intended to have the same meaning when used throughout the regulations.

The terms "agree" and "agreement" do not have the same meaning as "consent." These terms refer to an understanding between the parties, parent and school district personnel, on a given issue and need not be in writing unless a specific requirement calls for a written agreement (e.g., IEP Team attendance when members' area of curriculum or related services is not being modified or discussed in the meeting).

Q

If a school district gives parents the option of receiving prior written notice and procedural safeguards notices by electronic mail, what documentation is required and can parent consent be obtained by electronic or digital signatures?

A

If parents are given the option to receive notices electronically and elect to do so, documentation of the process is left up to the states and school districts that choose electronic communication.

States may also choose to permit the use of electronic or digital signatures for parental consent, as long as appropriate safeguards are taken to protect the integrity of the process.

Q *To what does the phrase "make reasonable efforts" refer when used in the context of obtaining parental consent for initial evaluation, initial provision of services, and reevaluation?*

A The phrase "make reasonable efforts" refers to a school district documenting its attempts to obtain parental consent. The specific procedures that a school district must use include keeping a record of its attempts, such as:

- Detailed records of telephone calls made or attempted and the results of those calls;

- Copies of correspondence sent to parents and any responses received; and

- Detailed records of visits made to the parent's home or place of residence and the results of those visits.

Q *What steps must a school district take in order to conduct an initial evaluation of a child to determine if the child qualifies as a child with a disability under Part B of IDEA?*

A A school district proposing to conduct an initial evaluation of a child in order to determine if the child qualifies under Part B must provide the parent written prior notice and procedural safeguards notice consistent with the Part B requirements, and obtain informed parental consent before conducting the evaluation.

Q *What are the specific requirements for obtaining parental consent for initial evaluation if a child is a ward of the state?*

A For initial evaluations only, if the child is a ward of the state and is not residing with the child's parent, the school district is not required to obtain informed consent from the parent of the child to determine whether the child is a child with a disability if:

- Despite reasonable efforts to do so, the district cannot discover the whereabouts of the parent of the child;

- The rights of the parents of the child have been terminated in accordance with state law; and

- The rights of the parent to make educational decisions have been subrogated by a judge in accordance with state law and consent for an initial evaluation has been given by an individual appointed by the judge to represent the child.

Q

Can employees of SEAs, school districts, or other state agencies, such as teachers, related service providers, or social workers initiate a request for an initial evaluation of a child to determine if the child is a child with a disability under Part B of IDEA?

A

Unless an employer is acting for a public agency, the answer is no. Although this is a rather narrow interpretation of Part B of IDEA 2004, it does not apply to the child find requirements. Employees, such as teachers or related service providers can still refer a child for evaluation; however, the parent of a child or public agency has the responsibility to initiate the evaluation process.

Q

What is the timeframe for conducting an initial evaluation of a child to determine if a child qualifies as a child with a disability under Part B of IDEA?

A

In general, a public agency has 60 days from receipt of parental consent for initial evaluation to conduct the evaluation, unless the SEA has established another timeframe for completing the process. However there are exceptions to meeting this timeframe.

- The first exception involves a situation where a parent repeatedly fails or refuses to produce the child for the evaluation.

- The second exception occurs when a child enrolls in a school of another public agency after the timeframe begins, but prior to determining if a child qualifies under Part B. The second exception only applies if the subsequent public agency is making sufficient progress to ensure a prompt completion of the evaluation within a specific time period agreed on by the public agency and the parent.

Q

Can the timeframe for conducting an initial evaluation of a child for determining the need for special education and related services be extended by mutual agreement of the parent and school district?

A

If a state uses the Part B 60-day timeframe within which the initial evaluation must be conducted, the timeframe cannot be extended by mutual agreement of the parties.

If a state adopts its own timeframe within which the initial evaluation must be conducted, a state could allow for an extension if the parent and school district mutually agree to one.

Q

How have the basic procedures for conducting an evaluation changed?

A

Two major changes were made in the final Part B regulations.

- One was the deletion of the reference to materials and procedures used to assess a child with limited English proficiency. This was replaced with the requirement that assessments and other evaluation materials "are provided and administered in the child's native language or other mode of communication and in the form most likely to yield accurate information on what the child knows and can do academically, developmentally, and functionally, unless it is not feasible to so provide and administer."

- The second change was the addition of the following assurance: Assessments of children with disabilities who transfer from one school district to another school district in the same school year are coordinated with such children's prior and subsequent schools as necessary and as expeditiously as possible to ensure prompt completion of full evaluations.

Q

Is screening for the purpose of determining the appropriate instructional strategies for implementing the curriculum considered to be an evaluation for eligibility?

A

No. The screening of a student by a teacher or specialist to determine appropriate instructional strategies for curriculum implementation is not considered to be an evaluation for eligibility for special education and related services.

Screening is considered a rather quick and simple process used with groups of children. Furthermore, because screening is not considered an evaluation under Part B, parental consent is not required.

Q

Can a school district use the procedural safeguards (e.g., mediation or due process hearing procedures) to override a parent's refusal or failure to respond to a request for initial evaluation or reevaluation if a child is home schooled or placed in a private school at the parent's own expense?

A

No. A new requirement was added to the regulations which prevent a school district from overriding a parent's refusal or nonresponsiveness in case of home schooled or privately placed children at parent's expense. In addition, under these circumstances, a school district is not required to consider these children eligible for services under the "parentally placed" provisions.

Q

What are the LEA's obligations if a parent refuses or fails to respond to a request for consent to the initial provision of special education and related services to the child?

A

A parent has the ultimate responsibility to determine if their child receives special education and related services. If a parent fails to respond or refuses to consent to services, a local educational agency cannot use the dispute resolution procedures (i.e., mediation, due process hearing) in order to provide special education and related services to a child. Furthermore, an LEA is no longer responsible for providing the child with FAPE, including conducting an IEP meeting or developing an IEP. These new provisions do not relieve an LEA of its responsibilities to provide the student with an education under state law and NCLB. Moreover, in order to meet the reasonable efforts requirement, an LEA must document its attempts to obtain parental consent.

Q

Under what conditions and how often must an LEA conduct a reevaluation of a child with a disability?

A

The conditions under which a reevaluation must be conducted include:

- If the LEA determines that the educational or related services needs, including improved academic achievement and functional performance of the child warrants a reevaluation; or

- If the child's parents or teacher requests a reevaluation.

The frequency for when a reevaluation must occur include:

- Not more frequently than once a year, unless the parent and the LEA agree otherwise; and

- At least once every 3 years, unless the parent and the LEA agree that a reevaluation is unnecessary.

Q

Do the final regulations change the requirement that an LEA evaluate a child with a disability before determining the child is no longer eligible for special education and related services?

A

Yes. Although the exceptions to conducting an evaluation due to graduation from secondary school with a regular diploma, or exceeding age eligibility for FAPE were in the IDEA 1997 regulations, they are now codified in the law. Furthermore, under these two circumstances, a new provision has been added as follows: an LEA shall provide the child with a summary of the child's academic achievement and functional performance, which shall include recommendations on how to assist the child in meeting the child's postsecondary goals.

IDENTIFYING CHILDREN WITH SPECIFIC LEARNING DISABILITIES

What are the new procedures for identifying children with specific learning disabilities?

A State must adopt criteria, which LEAs are required to use for determining whether a child has a specific learning disability. These criteria are:

- Must not require the use of a severe discrepancy between intellectual ability and achievement;

- Must permit the use of a process based on the child's response to scientific, research-based interventions; and

- May permit the use of other alternative research-based procedures.

What are the criteria for determining the existence of a specific learning disability?

The group may determine that a child has a specific learning disability if:

- The child does not achieve adequately for the child's age or to meet State-approved grade level standards in one or more of the listed areas when provided with learning experiences and instruction appropriate for the child's age or State-approved grade level standards. The list remains the same as IDEA 1997, with the addition of "reading fluency skills" and a change from mathematics "reasoning" to mathematics "problem solving."

- The child does not make sufficient progress to meet age or State-approved grade level standards in one or more of the listed areas when using a process based on the child's response to scientific, research-based intervention; or

- The child exhibits a pattern of strengths and weaknesses in performance, achievements, or both, relative to age, State-approved grade level standards, or intellectual development, determined by the group to be relevant to the identification of a specific learning disability based upon appropriate assessments; and

- The group determines that findings under the provisions above are not primarily the result of a visual, hearing, or motor disability; mental retardation; emotional disturbance; cultural factors; environmental or economic disadvantage; or limited English proficiency.

- To ensure that underachievement in a child suspected of having a specific learning disability is not due to lack of appropriate instruction in reading or math, the group must consider as part of the evaluation:

– Data demonstrating that prior to, or as part of the referral process, the child received appropriate instruction in general education settings provided by qualified personnel; and

– Data-based documentation provided to the child's parents of repeated assessments of achievement at reasonable intervals that reflect formal assessment of the child's progress during instruction.

• The LEA must promptly request parental consent to evaluate the child for special education and related services:

– If, prior to a referral, the child has not made adequate progress after an appropriate period of time when provided with appropriate instruction by qualified personnel; and

– Whenever a child is referred for an evaluation.

What is the description of the required observation?

The description of the required observation is as follows:

• The LEA must ensure that the child is observed in the child's learning environment to document academic performance and behavior in the area of difficulty. (IDEA 2004 deleted reference to a team member "other than the child's regular teacher.")

• In determining whether the child has a specific learning disability, the group must decide to use the information:

– From an observation of routine classroom instruction and monitoring of the child's performance before the referral for evaluation; or

– Must conduct observations.

What documentation is required for the eligibility determination?

New regulations:

• Eliminate the requirement of a severe discrepancy between achievement and ability; and

• Require that documentation include statements about the group's determination plus a statement about the following:

– If the child has participated in a process assessing the child's response to scientific, research-based interventions,

♦ The instructional strategies used and student-centered data collected;

♦ Documentation that the child's parents were notified about:

-- State policies on the amount and type of student performance data to be collected and the general education services to be provided;

-- Strategies for increasing the child's rate of learning; and

-- The parents' right to request an evaluation.

INDIVIDUALIZED EDUCATION PROGRAMS AND DEVELOPMENT OF THE IEP

Q

Do IEPs have to include both academic and functional goals?

A

Yes. The IDEA 2004 final regulations replaced a statement of present levels of educational performance with present levels of academic achievement and functional performance.

Q

How do IEPs address measurable annual goals?

A

The IDEA 2004 final regulations replaced a statement of measurable annual goals, including benchmarks or short-term objectives with a statement of measurable annual goals, including academic and functional goals. In the Comments and Analysis of the IDEA 2004 final regulations, the Department of Education states that, "a State that chooses to require benchmarks or short-term objectives in IEPs in that State would have to identify in writing to the LEAs located in the State and to the Secretary [of Education] that such rule, regulation, or policy is a State-imposed requirement, which is not required by Part B of the Act or the Federal regulations."

In addition, the IDEA 2004 final regulations added a statement detailing that children who take the alternate assessment aligned to alternate standards description of benchmarks or short-term objectives needs to be included in their IEP.

Q

How has the IEP statement regarding parental notification changed?

A

Although the IDEA 2004 final regulations do include a description of when periodic reports on the progress the child is making toward meeting the annual goals (such as through the use of quarterly or other periodic reports) will be provided, it deleted the statement "at least as often as parents are informed of their nondisabled children's progress."

Q

Do the special education and related services outlined in the IEP have to be based on peer-reviewed research?

A

Yes. In the IDEA 2004 final regulations, the IEP must include a statement that special education, related services, and supplementary aids and services are to be passed on peer-reviewed research, to the extent practicable, to be provided to the child, or on behalf of the child.

In the Comments and Analysis section of the IDEA 2004 regulations, the U.S. Department of Education stated that there is no single definition of "peer reviewed research" because the review process varies depending on the type of information to be reviewed. Additionally, the Department stated that it was beyond the scope of the IDEA regulations to define "peer reviewed research."

Q

How has the IEP statement concerning state and districtwide assessments changed?

A

The IDEA 2004 final regulations revised language regarding state and districtwide assessments to now read:

- A statement of any individual appropriate accommodations that are necessary to measure the academic achievement and functional performance of the child on State and districtwide assessments consistent with section 612(a)(16) of the Act; and

- If the IEP Team determines that the child must take an alternate assessment instead of a particular regular state or districtwide assessment of student achievement, a statement of why the child cannot participate in the regular assessment; and the particular alternate assessment selected is appropriate for the child.

Additional regulations relating to these provisions and their overlap with pending regulations under the Elementary and Secondary Education Act (ESEA) will be released by the Department of Education at a future date. CEC will notify its membership of this release.

Q

At what age must the IEP include statement of transition services?

A

The IDEA 2004 final regulations revised the statement on transition services to now be reflected on a child's IEP not later than the first IEP when the child turns 16, or younger if determined by the IEP Team.

Previously this age was 14. In addition the IEP must include the following:

- Appropriate measurable postsecondary goals based upon age appropriate transition assessments related to training, education, employment, and where appropriate, independent living skills; and

- The transition services (including courses of study) needed to assist the child in reaching those goals.

Q

A

Can SEAs and LEAs add additional requirements beyond what the Federal government directs?

Yes. The IDEA 2004 final regulations added language to reflect that the public agency does not have to include additional information in a child's IEP beyond what is explicitly required in IDEA 2004. In the Analysis and Comments, the Department of Education states, "There is nothing in the Act that limits States and LEAs from adding elements to the IEP, so long as the elements are not inconsistent with the Act or these regulations, and States do not interpret the Act to require these additional elements. However, if a State requires IEPs to include information beyond that which is explicitly required...the State must identify in writing to its LEAs and the Secretary that it is a State-imposed requirement and not one based on the Act or these regulations..."

Q

A

How do the regulations make changes to the IEP when considering transition services?

If a purpose of the IEP Team meeting will be consideration of the postsecondary goals for the child and the transition services needed to assist the child in reaching those goals, the public agency must invite the child with a disability and must take other steps to ensure that the child's preferences and interests are considered if the child is unable to attend the meeting, as was required previously.

To the extent appropriate, now with the consent of the parent or a child who has reached the age or majority, in implementing the requirements detailed previously, the public agency must invite a representative of any participating agency that is likely to be responsible for providing or paying for transition services. In the Comments and Analysis section, the Department explains that the addition of the consent provision was to specifically address issues related to the confidentiality of information.

In addition, IDEA 2004 deleted the previous requirement that stated, "If an agency invited to send a representative to a meeting does not do so, the public agency shall take other steps to obtain participation of the other agency in the planning of any transition services." In the

Comments and Analysis section, the Department states that IDEA has never given public agencies the authority to compel other agencies to participate in the planning of transition services for a child with a disability.

Q
A

Can a member of the IEP Team be excused from an IEP Team meeting if their responsibilities are not being discussed?

Yes. IEP Team members are not required to attend an IEP Team meeting, in whole or in part, if the parent of a child with a disability and the public agency agree, in writing, that the attendance of the member is not necessary because the member's area of the curriculum or related services is not being modified or discussed in the meeting.

In the Comments and Analysis section, the Department differentiates between "agreement" and "consent" by stating "an agreement is not the same as consent, but instead refers to an understanding between the parent and the LEA [local education agency]".

Q
A

If the responsibilities of an IEP Team member are to be discussed during an IEP Team meeting, can that Team member be excused?

Yes. A member of the IEP Team may be excused from attending an IEP Team meeting, in whole or in part, when the meeting involves a modification to or discussion of the member's area of curriculum or related services if:

• The parent, in writing, and the public agency consent to the excusal; and

• The member submits, in writing to the parent and the IEP Team, input into the development of the IEP prior to the meeting.

In the Comments and Analysis section, the Department explains that the definition of consent required a parent to be fully informed of all information relevant to the activity for which consent is sought and requires a parent to agree in writing.

Q
A

Does the new law address if the IEP Team should include the IDEA Part C service coordinator or other representatives of the system?

Yes, in the case of a child who was previously served under Part C, an invitation to the initial IEP Team meeting must, at the request of the parent, be sent to the Part C service coordinator or other representatives of the Part C system to assist with the smooth transition of services.

Q *What responsibility, if any, does the LEA have with regard to the individualized family services plan of a preschooler if they are transferring from the Part C program to Part B?*

A In the case of a preschool child with a disability, the IEP Team must consider the child's individualized family services plan (IFSP) that contains the IFSP content required under Part C, including the natural environments statement.

Q *Have there been any changes to the notification requirements a public agency must provide to parents prior to an IEP Team meeting when children are transferring from Part C to Part B?*

A Yes, in addition to previous notice requirements, parents must be informed of their right to have the Part C service coordinator or other representatives of the Part C system invited to participate in the initial IEP Team meeting for a child previously served under Part C.

Q *If a child with an IEP moves from one school district to another, but within the same state, does the new school district have to honor the child's IEP?*

A If a child with a disability (who had an IEP that was in effect in a previous public agency in the same state) transfers to a new public agency in the same state, and enrolls in a new school within the same school year, the new public agency (in consultation with the parents) must provide FAPE to the child (including services comparable to those described in the child's IEP from the previous public agency), until the new public agency either:

- Adopts the child's IEP from the previous public agency; or

- Develops, adopts, and implements a new IEP.

In the Comments and Analysis section, the Department declined to define the term "comparable" and instead stated that the Department interprets "comparable" to have the plain meaning of the word, which is "similar" or "equivalent."

Q *If a child with an IEP moves from one state to another, does the new state of residence have to honor the child's IEP?*

A If a child with a disability (who had an IEP that was in effect in a previous public agency in another state) transfers to a pubic agency in a new state, and enrolls in a new school within the same school year, the new public agency (in consultation with the parents) must provide the child with FAPE (including services comparable to those described in the child's IEP from the previous public agency), until the new public agency:

- Conducts an evaluation (if determined by the new public agency); and

- Develops, adopts, and implements a new IEP, if appropriate.

In the Comments and Analysis section, the Department addresses the question that the regulations should clarify what happens when a child transfers to a state with eligibility criteria that are different from the previous state's criteria. The Department states that the new public agency must determine if an evaluation is necessary to determine whether the child is a child with a disability under the new public agency's criteria. Until the evaluation is conducted, the new public agency must provide, in consultation with the parent, FAPE including comparable services.

Can changes be made to an IEP without holding an IEP Team meeting?

In making changes to a child's IEP after the annual IEP Team meeting for a school year, the parent of a child with a disability and the public agency may agree not to convene an IEP Team meeting for the purposes of making those changes, and instead may develop a written document to amend or modify that child's current IEP. If changes are made to an IEP in this way, the public agency must inform members of the IEP Team of the changes.

Does IDEA 2004 make any changes regarding the consolidation of IEP Team meetings?

Yes, to the extent possible, the public agency must encourage the consolidation of reevaluation meeting for the child and other IEP Team meetings for the child.

Can amendments be made to an IEP?

Yes, amendments can be made to an IEP either by the entire IEP Team at an IEP Team meeting, or by not convening a meeting (see previous question). Changes can be made by amending the IEP rather than by redrafting the entire IEP. Upon request, a parent must be provided with a revised copy of the IEP with the amendments incorporated.

Q *Can IEP Team members use alternative means of participation (i.e., conference calls) for an IEP Team meeting?*

A Yes. When conducting IEP Team meetings and placement meetings and administrative matters (such as scheduling, exchange of witness lists, and status conferences), the parent of a child with a disability and a public agency may agree to use alternative means of meeting participation such as video conferences and conference calls.

Q *What is the purpose of the multiyear IEP demonstration pilot program?*

A The new law states that the purpose of the pilot is to provide an opportunity for not more than 15 states to allow parents and LEAs the opportunity for long-term planning by offering the option of developing a comprehensive multiyear IEP, not to exceed 3 years, that is designed to coincide with the natural transition points for the child.

Q *What are natural transition points?*

A The term "natural transition points" means those periods that are close in time to the transition of a child with a disability from preschool to elementary grades from elementary grades to middle or junior high school grades, from middle or junior high school grades to secondary school grades, and from secondary school grades to postsecondary activities, but in no case a period longer than 3 years.

Q *In a state's proposal for implementing a multiyear IEP pilot program, what are the required components?*

A The following components are required in a state's proposal:

• Reducing the paperwork burden on teachers, principals, administrators, and related service providers; and non-instructional time spent by teachers;

• Enhancing longer-term educational planning;

• Improving positive outcomes for children with disabilities;

• Promoting collaboration between IEP Team members; and

• Ensuring satisfaction of family members.

PROCEDURAL SAFEGUARDS: DUE PROCESS PROCEDURES FOR PARENTS AND CHILDREN

Q

Do the regulations address how often a parent is entitled to an independent educational evaluation at public expense?

A

Yes. A new provision was added to the regulations which states that, "A parent is entitled to only one independent educational evaluation at public expense each time the public agency conducts an evaluation with which the parent disagrees."

Q

How often and when must a school district give parents a copy of the procedural safeguards notice?

A

The timing for providing parents with a copy of their procedural safeguards has changed in the regulations. Now, a school district is only required to provide parents a copy one time per school year and under the following situations:

* At initial referral or if a parent requests an evaluation;

* Upon receipt of the first state complaint or first due process complaint in a school year;

* As required under the discipline procedures; and

* If a parent requests a copy.

The provisions under the IDEA 1997 regulations that required a school district to give parents a copy of their procedural safeguards "upon each notification of an IEP meeting and upon reevaluation of the child" were deleted.

Q

If a school district elects to post the procedural safeguards notice on the district's Web site, how does this impact a district's obligation to provide parents with a copy of this notice?

A

As noted by the U.S. Department of Education in its discussion of this issue, a school district does not meet its obligation to provide parents with a copy of their procedural safeguards by sending them to a Web site. The parent must be offered a printed copy of the notice. The Department does go on to provide additional guidance by stating that, "if, however, a parent declines the offered printed copy of the notice and indicates a clear preference to obtain the notice electronically on their own from the agency's Web site, it would be reasonable for the public agency to document that it offered a printed copy of the notice that the parent declined."

Q
A

What changes were made to the contents of the procedural safeguards notice?

There were multiple changes made to the notice including:

- Adding references to the time periods for filing complaints and civil actions;

- Providing an agency with the opportunity to resolve the complaint; and

- Requiring a description of the difference between a due process complaint and state complaint including the jurisdiction of each, issues that may be raised, and timelines for filing and making decisions.

Q
A

What major changes were made to the procedures for establishing and implementing a "mediation" process by a school district?

There were multiple changes made to the mediation process including:

- Providing for the use of mediation for "matters arising prior to the filing of" a due process complaint;

- Giving the opportunity to both parents and schools, on an optional basis, that choose not to use mediation to meet with a disinterested third party to resolve the issue;

- Adding provisions to the mediation agreement that make it legally binding, that require that it be signed by both parties, and that it be enforceable in court; and

- Deleting the optional signing of a confidentiality pledge prior to conducting mediation.

Q
A

What is the timeline for filing a due process complaint? And are there any exceptions to this timeline?

Unless state law establishes a specific timeline for filing a complaint, the final 2004 regulations provides for the filing of a complaint on an alleged violation "that occurred not more than two years before the date the parent or public agency knew or should have known about the alleged action that forms the basis of the due process complaint." A timeline specified under state law may be shorter or longer than the 2-year time limitation established under Part B regulations.

The time limitations described above shall not apply if the parent was prevented from requesting the hearing due to:

- Specific misrepresentations by the local educational agency that it had resolved the problem forming the basis of the complaint; or

- The local educational agency's withholding of information from the parent that was required under Part B to be provided to the parent.

Q
A

What changes were made to the due process complaint procedures including the content of the notice?

Several significant changes were made to the procedures including:

- Requiring "either party," parent or school district, or the party's attorney, to provide the other party with a copy of the complaint. (The complaint continues to remain confidential.)

- Forwarding a copy of the complaint to the SEA by the party filing the complaint.

- Restricting either party's right to a hearing until the party files a due process complaint that meets the required content provisions.

- Adding contact information and name of school child is attending to required content of complaint for homeless children or youth.

Q
A

What are the required procedures for determining whether a due process complaint notice is sufficient (i.e., meets the content requirements under the Part B regulations)?

If the party, parent, or school district, receiving the due process complaint believes that it does not meet the content requirements specified in the regulations, the receiving party, within 15 days of

receipt of the complaint, must notify the hearing officer and sending party, in writing, of this belief.

The hearing officer, within 5 days of receipt of the above notification, must determine on the face of the complaint whether it meets the content requirements and notify both parties, in writing, of his or her decision.

Q
A

Under what conditions can a party, parent, or school district amend its due process complaint?

There are only two situations where a party may amend its due process complaint.

- If the other party consents in writing to the amendment and is given the opportunity to resolve the complaint through a resolution meeting; or

- If the hearing officer grants permission to amend the complaint at any time not later than 5 days before the beginning of a due process hearing.

Furthermore, it should be noted that with the filing of an amended due process complaint, the timelines for conducting a resolution meeting and time period for resolving the complaint begin again.

Q
A

What are the obligations of the school district and "receiving party" to respond to a due process complaint?

The following provisions apply when responding to a due process complaint:

- If the district has not sent a prior written notice to the parent regarding the subject matter contained in the parent's due process complaint notice, the district shall within 10 days of receiving the complaint, send to the parent a response that includes:

  - An explanation of why the district proposed or refused to take the action raised in the complaint;

  - A description of other options that the IEP Team considered and the reasons why those options were rejected;

  - A description of each evaluation procedure, assessment, record, or report the district used as the basis for the proposed or refused action; and

  - A description of the factors that are relevant to the district's proposal or refusal.

- A response filed by a school district shall not be construed to preclude the district from asserting that the parent's due process complaint notice was insufficient where appropriate.

- Except as provided above, the party receiving the complaint must, within 10 days of its receipt, send to the other party a response specifically addressing the issues raised.

Q
A

What is the purpose of conducting a resolution meeting?

The meeting gives parents a chance to talk about their concerns and the basis for the complaint, so that the district has an opportunity to resolve the issue.

Q *Who are the participants in a resolution meeting?*

A In general, participants in the meeting include the parent, a representative of the district who has decision-making authority, and a knowledgeable member or members of the IEP Team, as determined by both parties to the complaint. In addition, if the parent brings an attorney to the meeting, the district may have an attorney there also.

Q *Are there any circumstances under which a resolution meeting is not required?*

A A resolution meeting does not have to be held if the parent and district agree, in writing, to waive the meeting or agree to mediation.

Q *What option does a school district have if a parent refuses to participate in a resolution meeting?*

A If after making reasonable efforts and documenting these efforts to obtain parental participation in a resolution meeting, a district is unable to convince the parent to attend the meeting, the complaint may be dismissed. Under these conditions, at the end of the 30-day resolution period, a district may request that a hearing officer dismiss the parent's complaint.

Q *What options does a parent have if a district does not convene or refuses to participate in a resolution meeting?*

A If a district does not hold a resolution meeting within 15 days of the parent's due process complaint notice, or does not participate in the meeting, the parent may ask the hearing officer to start the due process hearing timeline.

Q *Under what conditions can the 30-day resolution period be adjusted in order to begin the timeline for a due process hearing?*

A The regulations describe three situations where the 45-day timeline for conducting a hearing begins relative to the resolution meeting process. These include:

- Both parties agree in writing to waive the resolution meeting;

- After either the mediation or resolution meeting starts, but before the end of the 30-day period, the parties agree in writing that no agreement is possible; or

- If both parties agree in writing to continue the mediation at end of the 30-day resolution period, but later, the parent or public agency withdrawals from the mediation process.

The 45-day timeline for a due process hearing begins the day after one of the situations described previously.

Q
A

What requirements apply to a "written settlement agreement" reached at a resolution meeting?

If the issue(s) in dispute is resolved at the meeting, a legally binding written agreement must be developed. Both parties, the parent and the district representative who has the authority to bind the district, must sign the agreement, and the agreement must be enforceable in court or through other available state enforcement procedures. Either party, parent or district representative, may void the agreement within 3 business days of its execution.

Q
A

What requirements apply to a hearing officer's decision in a due process hearing?

The regulations add specific requirements regarding a hearing officer's decision. These include:

- Basing a decision on whether a child received FAPE on substantive grounds.

- Adding criteria when a procedural violation is the basis for determining whether a child received FAPE only if procedural inadequacies:

  - Impeded the child's right to a FAPE;

  - Significantly impeded the parent's opportunity to participate in the decision-making process regarding the provision of a FAPE to the parent's child; or

  - Caused a deprivation of educational benefit.

- Noting that the previous procedures do not keep a hearing officer from ordering a school district to comply with the procedural safeguards requirement.

Q
A

What changes were made to the requirement that an SEA develop model forms for filing a complaint?

There were multiple changes made to this provision including:

- Adding references to assisting parents and "other parties" in filing a "state complaint." (Previously the requirement only addressed parents filing a "due process complaint".)

- Clarifying that the SEA or school district may not require the use of these model forms.

- Allowing parents, districts, or other parties to use the model forms, another form, or document as long as they meet the content requirements for filing a due process or state complaint.

Q
A

What changes were made to the "pendency" requirements in an administrative or judicial proceeding regarding a due process complaint?

There were significant changes made to the pendency requirements in the regulations including:

- Adding the phrase "A due process complaint notice requesting" a due process hearing to the pendency language. In its discussion of this revision, the U.S. Department of Education noted, "This change is needed to clarify that a child's right to remain in the current educational placement attaches when a due process complaint is filed, regardless of whether the due process complaint results in a request for a due process hearing."

- Clarifying pendency for a child transitioning from the Part C system by adding the following provision, "If the complaint involves an application for initial services under the part from a child who is transitioning from Part C of the Act to Part B and is no longer eligible for Part C services because the child has turned three, the public agency is not required to provide the Part C services that the child has been receiving. If the child is found eligible for special education and related services under Part B and the parent consents to the initial provision of special education and related services, under §300.300 (b), then the public agency must provide those special education and related services that are not in dispute between the parent and the public agency."

- Removing the phrase "or local agency" from the pendency provision that when a hearing officer's or a state review official's decision agrees with the parents that a change of placement is appropriate, that placement is treated as an agreement between the state and parent for purposes of determining the child's current placement during subsequent appeals. This change was based on longstanding judicial interpretation of pendency in case law.

Q

Is there a time limit for bringing a civil action once a hearing officer or a state review official has rendered a decision in a due process hearing?

A

Yes. The party bringing the action shall have 90 days from the date of the decision of the hearing officer or a state review official to bring such an action, or, if the state has an explicit time limitation for bringing such action under Part B in such time as the state law allows.

Q

Can a court award reasonable attorneys' fees to an SEA or LEA who is the prevailing party in an action or proceeding brought under the procedural safeguards provisions in Part B?

A

Yes. In any action or proceeding brought under section 615 of the Act, the court, in its discretion, may award reasonable attorneys' fees as part of the costs to a prevailing:

- Party who is a state educational agency or local educational agency against the attorney of a parent who files a complaint or subsequent cause of action that is frivolous, unreasonable, or without foundation, or against the attorney of a parent who continued to litigate after the litigation clearly became frivolous, unreasonable, or without foundation; or

- State educational agency or local educational agency against the attorney of a parent, or against the parent, if the parent's complaint or subsequent cause of action was presented for any improper purpose, such as to harass, to cause unnecessary delay, or to needlessly increase the cost of litigation.

Q

Can attorneys' fees be awarded for a resolution session?

A

No. A resolution session is not considered a meeting convened as a result of an administrative hearing or judicial action, or an administrative hearing or judicial action for purposes of awarding attorneys' fees.

What changes were made to the surrogate parent requirement under procedural safeguards?

In addition to revising the definition of parent, adding a definition of ward of the state, and address parental consent for initial evaluation for a ward of the state, all of which impact the surrogate parent requirement, four additional provisions were added as follows:

- A reference to unaccompanied homeless youth was added to the list of children whose rights are to be protected;

- In the case of a child who is:

  - A ward of the state, the judge overseeing the case may appoint the surrogate parent, if the surrogate meets the employee disclaimers; and

  - An unaccompanied homeless youth, appropriate staff of emergency shelters, transitional shelters, independent living programs, and street outreach programs, regardless of their status as an employee may be temporarily appointed as a surrogate until a person who meets all the criteria is appointed.

- The SEA shall make reasonable efforts to ensure the assignment of a surrogate no more than 30 days after there is a determination by the district that the child needs a surrogate.

DISCIPLINE PROCEDURES

Do the final Part B regulations provide clarification on the phrase "consider any unique circumstances on a case-by-case basis" when determining whether a change of placement is appropriate?

No. The final regulations are silent on this topic. School personnel at the local level are in the best position to determine any unique circumstances that may exist in any given case. Factors that school personnel may want to consider in making their decision could include:

- A child's discipline history;

- A child's ability to understand consequences;

- A child's expression of remorse; and

- Support provided to the child prior to violating a code of student conduct.

Q

Do "in-school suspension" or "bus suspension" count as a part of the days of suspension in determining the disciplinary actions that school personnel may take when a child with a disability violates a code of student conduct?

A

The final Part B regulations do not address in-school or bus suspension. However, the analysis of comments and changes section of the regulations offers the following guidance:

- "...in school suspension would not be considered a part of the days of suspension...as long as the child is afforded the opportunity to continue to appropriately participate in the general curriculum, continue to receive the services specified on the child's IEP, and continue to participate to the extent they would have in their current placement." Portions of a school day that a child had been suspended may be considered as a removal in regard to determining whether there is a pattern of removals..."

- "Whether a bus suspension would count as a day of suspension would depend on whether the bus transportation is a part of a child's IEP. If the bus transportation were a part of the child's IEP, the bus suspension would be treated as a suspension...unless the public agency provides the bus service in some other way, because that transportation is necessary for the child to obtain access to the location where services will be delivered. If the bus transportation is not a part of the child's IEP, a bus suspension is not a suspension..."

Q

What constitutes a change of placement because of disciplinary removals?

A

A change of placement under the discipline procedures occurs if:

- A child with a disability is removed from the child's current educational placement for more than 10 consecutive school days; or

- The child has been subjected to a series of removals that constitute a pattern.

Q

What requirements apply in determining whether a series of removals constitutes a pattern resulting in a change of placement under the discipline provisions?

A

There is a three-part test for determining a pattern:

- "The series of removals total more than 10 school days in a school year";

- "The child's behavior is substantially similar to the child's behavior in previous incidents that resulted in the series of removals"; and

- "Because of such additional factors as the length of each removal, the total amount of time the child has been removed, and the proximity of the removals to one another."

Decisions are to be made on a case-by-case basis and are reviewable under the due process and judicial procedures.

When is a school district required to hold a meeting for the purpose of making a "manifestation determination" and who are the participants at the meeting?

A meeting for making a manifestation determination must be held within 10 school days of any decision to change a child's placement under the discipline procedures. The participants at the meeting include: the school district, the parent, and relevant members of the child's IEP team, as determined by both parties.

What are the criteria used to determine whether a child's conduct is a manifestation of the child's disability?

Significant revisions were made to the IDEA 1997 statute as a result of the reauthorization process. In the IDEA 2004 statute, Congress removed the requirements regarding a child's ability to control or understand the consequences or impact of the behavior and the appropriateness of the placement, including the implementation of the IEP and identified services.

The criteria in the final Part B regulations now require the group making the decision to determine:

- If the conduct in question was caused by, or had a direct and substantial relationship to the child's disability; or

- If the conduct in question was the direct result of the LEA's failure to implement the IEP.

- If either of the previous criteria are met, the conduct must be determined to be a manifestation of the child's disability.

- If the group determines that the LEA failed to implement the IEP, the LEA must take immediate steps to remedy those deficiencies.

What are the requirements for conducting a functional behavioral assessment (FBA) and implementing a behavioral intervention plan (BIP) under the discipline procedures?

The requirements under IDEA 1997 for conducting a FBA and implementing a BIP were significantly changed by IDEA 2004. As noted by the U.S. Department of Education in its discussion of the changes made to these requirements "Congress specifically removed from the Act a requirement to conduct a functional behavioral assessment or review and modify an existing behavioral intervention plan for all children within 10 days of a disciplinary removal, regardless of whether the behavior was a manifestation or not." The department also made the point that separate from the discipline procedures, a BIP could be addressed by the IEP team through a child's IEP.

Under the final Part B regulations, the IEP team is only required to address the FBA and BIP provisions when there is a change of placement and the child's behavior was determined to be a manifestation of the child's disability. In those situations where a change of placement is for more than 10 consecutive school days and the child's behavior is not a manifestation of the child's disability or removal is for weapons, drugs, or serious bodily injury, the IEP team only addresses the FBA and BIP provisions "as appropriate" in an attempt to keep the behavior from occurring again.

Q
What major changes were made to the requirements under "special circumstances" (e.g., weapons, drugs) in the final Part B regulations?

A
There were several significant changes made to these requirements including:

- Changing the 45 "calendar" day timeline for removals to 45 "school" days without regard to whether the child's behavior is a manifestation of the child's disability.

- Adding "serious bodily injury" as a special circumstance.

Q
What is the definition of "serious bodily injury"?

A
The term means bodily injury that involves a substantial risk of death, extreme physical pain, protracted and obvious disfigurement, or protracted loss or impairment of the function of a bodily member, organ, or mental faculty.

Q
What changes were made to the "stay-put" (placement during appeals) provision in the final Part B regulations under the discipline procedures?

A
The stay-put provision that applied to the disciplinary procedures under IDEA 1997 statute was changed by the IDEA 2004 statute. In its discussion of this provision, in the analysis of comments and changes section of the final Part B regulations, the U.S. Department of Education stated, "in light of Congress' clear intent that, when there is an appeal...by the parent or the public agency, the child shall remain

in the interim alternative educational setting chosen by the IEP team pending the hearing officer's decision or until the time period for the disciplinary action expires, whichever occurs first, unless the parent and the public agency agree otherwise."

Any change in the time period that a child must remain in the interim alternative education setting (IAES) may be made by the parent and the public agency, not the IEP team. The IEP team is responsible for determining the IAES, not for establishing the time period that the child remains in that setting.

Q

What are the timelines for conducting an expedited due process hearing, including issuing a final decision, holding a resolution meeting, and the right of appeal?

A

In general, an expedited due process hearing "must occur within 20 school days of the date the complaint requesting the hearing is filed," and a decision is made by the hearing officer" within 10 school days after the hearing."

The procedures for holding a resolution meeting also apply with modified timelines and include waiving the meeting or agreeing to mediation. There is a 7-day timeline for holding a resolution meeting and a 15-day timeline for proceeding with the hearing unless the parties have resolved the issue(s).

Finally, the timelines for appealing a hearing officer's decision apply in the case of an expedited due process hearing. This would include a 30-day timeline if the SEA has an impartial review process, and a 90-day timeline or state established time limitation for filing a civil action.

Q

What changes were made to the "basis of knowledge" requirements related to protections for children not yet eligible for special education and related services?

A

There were multiple changes made to this requirement, including the deletion of the phrase "unless the parent is illiterate or has a disability that prevents compliance" regarding written notification and the phrase "the behavior or performance of the child demonstrates the need for such service." The new requirement now indicates that:

- "A public agency must be deemed to have knowledge that a child with a disability if, before the behavior that precipitated the disciplinary action occurred:

- The parent of the child has expressed concern in writing to supervisory or administrative personnel of the appropriate educational agency, or a teacher of the child, that the child is in need of special education and related services;

- The parent of the child has requested an evaluation of the child pursuant to Part B; or

- The teacher of the child, or other personnel of the local educational agency, expressed specific concerns about a pattern of behavior demonstrated by the child, directly to the director of special education of the agency or to other supervisory personnel of the agency.

A public agency would not be deemed to have knowledge that the child is a child with a disability...if the parent of the child has not allowed an evaluation of the child pursuant to Part B evaluation procedures or has refused services under Part B or the child has been evaluated... and it was determined that the child was not a child with a disability under Part B."

MONITORING AND ENFORCEMENT

Q

Do the states' monitoring and enforcement requirements apply to both Part B and Part C of IDEA 2004?

A

Yes, the monitoring and enforcement requirements outlined in the regulations do apply to both grants to states for children ages 3 to 21 (Part B) and the infants and toddlers with disabilities program ages birth to 2 (Part C). In the analysis of comments and changes section, the Department of Education addressed this issue by noting that, "Section 300.600 [state monitoring and enforcement] applies only to Part B of the Act. However, the commenters are correct that the monitoring and enforcement activities in section 616 of the Act also apply Part C, as provided in section 642 of the Act. The Department will address this recommendation in the promulgation of regulations implementing Part C of the Act."

Q

What is the primary emphasis of state monitoring?

A

The regulations state that the primary focus of a state's monitoring activities must be on improving educational results and functional outcomes for all students with disabilities and ensuring that public agencies meet the program requirements under IDEA 2004, with an emphasis on those requirements that are most closely related to improving educational results for children with disabilities.

Q

What are the states' responsibilities to monitor and enforce the implementation of IDEA 2004 requirements including reporting on state and local performance?

A

As part of its general supervisory responsibilities, a state must monitor LEAs and local early intervention programs using quantifiable and qualitative indicators established by the U.S. Secretary of the Department of Education in priority areas. This involves annually reporting on the performance of the state, LEAs and local early intervention programs on progress toward state performance plan targets. This also includes enforcement requirements under IDEA 2004.

The U.S. Secretary of the Department Education has identified quantifiable and qualitative indicators needed to measure state and local performance in the following priority areas:

- FAPE in the LRE;

- State implementation of its general supervisory responsibilities in child find, effective monitoring, resolution meetings, mediation, and a system of transition services; and

- Disproportionality in special education and related services by race and ethnicity resulting from inappropriate identification.

Q

What is a state performance plan (SPP) and an annual performance report for LEAs and early intervention programs?

A

Not later than December 3, 2005, each state must have had in place a performance plan that evaluates the state's efforts to implement the requirements and purposes of IDEA 2004 and describes how the state will improve such implementation.

- Each state must submit the state's performance plan to the Secretary for approval as described in section 616 of the Act;

- Each state must review its state performance plan at least once every 6 years, and submit any amendments to the Secretary; and

- As part of the state performance plan, each state must establish measurable and rigorous targets for the indicators established by the Secretary under the priority areas listed previously.

Each state must collect valid and reliable information as needed to report annually to the Secretary on the indicators established by the Secretary for the state performance plans.

If the Secretary permits states to collect data on specific indicators through state monitoring or sampling, the state must collect data on those indicators for each LEA at least once during the period of the state performance plan.

**Q
A**

How does the state use the targets established in the SPP to monitor and publicly report on the performance of LEAs?

Every year the state must report to the public on the performance of each LEA and local early intervention program located in the state concerning the targets in the state performance plan. In addition, the state must make the state's performance plan available through public means (e.g., posted on the Web site of the SEA, distribution to the media, and distribution through other public agencies).

If the state collects performance data though state monitoring or sampling, the state must include in its report the most recently available performance data on each LEA and local early intervention program, and the date the data was obtained.

The state must not report any information that would result in the disclosure of personally identifiable information about individual children.

**Q
A**

What are the requirements for making determinations of state and local performance as it relates to enforcement?

The regulations contain an extensive set of requirements for making determinations regarding state and local performance. It is done through the annual reporting of state and local data on the implementation of the SPP, determinations process, and enforcement procedures.

There are four distinct "determinations" spelled out in the regulations that apply to the state for use in determining the degree to which IDEA requirements are being implemented and applied to state and local programs. These include: (1) meets requirements, (2) needs assistance, (3) needs intervention, or (4) needs substantial intervention in implementing IDEA requirements.

If a state or a local entity does not "meet requirements" under IDEA, it will fall into one of the three remaining categories (e.g., needs assistance, needs intervention, or needs substantial intervention), which triggers a series of required enforcement actions. Within each of the categories of determinations, the federal government has specific actions it may impose on the state, that range from technical assistance to referral to the Justice Department (intermediate steps including the preparation of corrective action plans and withholding of funds).

If the Secretary takes an enforcement action against a state, the Secretary must report to Congress on the action taken and why enforcement was taken within 30 days.

Q

Is there any specific enforcement provision requiring states' action related to LEA maintenance of effort?

A

Yes. A state is required to prohibit an LEA from reducing its maintenance of effort in any given fiscal year, if the LEA does not meet the Part B requirements, including targets in the SPP.

AUTHORIZATION, ALLOTMENT, USE OF FUNDS, AUTHORIZATION OF APPROPRIATIONS

Q

What is IDEA full funding?

A

When the first federal special education law was passed in 1975, the Education for All Handicapped Children Act, Congress promised that the federal government would pay 40% of the excess cost of educating children with disabilities to relieve the financial burden on states and local school districts.

This additional 40% federal government contribution is referred to as full funding for Part B. It costs approximately twice as much to educate a child with disabilities as it does to educate a student without disabilities.

Although the 1975 law sought to reach that 40% federal contribution by 1981, in 2006 the federal share for educating children with disabilities is only 17%, less than half of what Congress promised 31 years ago.

CEC continues to advocate for IDEA to receive mandatory funding, like social security and Medicare, so that it would force Congress to provide funding at levels that would reach full funding by 2011. Currently, IDEA is a discretionary funded program, and as a result Congress funds IDEA programs annually.

Q

How much money was authorized for special education under IDEA 2004?

A

When Congress wrote IDEA 2004 (P.L. 108-446), it authorized funding IDEA at the following levels:

$12,358,376,571 for fiscal year 2005;

$14,648,647,143 for fiscal year 2006;

$16,938,917,714 for fiscal year 2007;

$19,229,188,286 for fiscal year 2008;

$21,519,458,857 for fiscal year 2009;

$23,809,729,429 for fiscal year 2010; and

$26,100,000,000 for fiscal year 2011;

Such sums as may be necessary for fiscal year 2012 and each succeeding fiscal year.

Unfortunately, Congress has not funded IDEA at the authorized levels above and as a result has decreased the federal commitment to special education.

Q

Why hasn't Congress fully funded IDEA?

A

Although the law of 1975 says that Congress will fully fund IDEA Part B, Congress is not even halfway toward doing so. Many members of Congress and Presidential administrations believe that making IDEA a mandatory spending program, like Social Security and Medicare, will put a drain on federal funds.

When Congress chooses not to fully fund IDEA, it puts a significant strain on already tight state and location education resources, and it also reneges on a promise Congress made over 31 years ago.

Q

What are the funding allocation formulas under the regulations?

A

The regulations provide formulas for determining the maximum amount a state can receive based on numerous factors, including the number of children receiving special education and related services ages 3 to 5 and 6 to 21, and average per-pupil expenditure in the United States, according to the fiscal year in effect. The regulations also provide a funding formula based on a state's relative population of children ages 3 to 21 with disabilities and based on the relative population of children with disabilities who are living in poverty. No state's allocation can be less than the previous year's allocation if the amount available for allocations to states for a fiscal year is equal to or granter than the amount allocated to states for the preceding fiscal year.

After 2006, the maximum grant will be 40% of annual per pupil expenditure (APPE) times the number of children with disabilities the state served in school year 2004 to 2005 adjusted by:

- The annual rate of change in the state's population of children ages 3 through 21 who are of the same age as children with disabilities for whom the state ensures the availability of FAPE (85% of the adjustment); and

- The state's children living in poverty in the same age range (15% of the adjustment).

Q

When a school wants to bill a public insurance company (e.g., Medicaid) for a child's services, does the school have to obtain parental consent every time the public insurance is accessed?

A

Yes. If a child with a disability is covered by public benefits or insurance, such as Medicaid, a school must obtain parental consent every time the public insurance is accessed to provide or pay for services.

In the Comments and Analysis section of the regulations, the Department states, "We believe obtaining parental consent each time the public agency seeks to use a parent's public insurance or other public benefits to provide or pay for a services is important to protect the privacy rights of the parent and to ensure that the parent is fully informed of a public agency's access to his or her public benefits or insurance and the services paid by the public benefits or insurance program."

However, in a January 23, 2007 letter to a superintendent in Florida, Alexa Posny, Director of OSEP in the U.S. Department of Education, stated, "We [U.S. Department of Education] believe that permitting a public agency to obtain parent consent for a specified amount of services for a specified period of time would be sufficient to enable parents to make an informed decision as to whether to consent before a public agency can access their or their child's public benefits or other public insurance."   The letter also indicates that this information is provided as informal guidance and is not legally binding, but represents interpretation by the U.S. Department of Education.

Q

Can a state use IDEA Part B funds to pay for state-law mandated obligations to LEAs?

A

No. The regulations clarify that a state may not use funds paid to it under IDEA Part B to satisfy state-law mandated funding obligations to LEAs, including funding based on student attendance or enrollment, or inflation.

In the Comments and Analysis section, the Department further clarifies that states with laws that require a specific level of funding to their LEAs cannot use Federal IDEA Part B funds for this purpose.

Q

What changes have been made to the exceptions to maintenance of effort by an LEA?

A

In certain situations, the LEA may reduce the level of expenditures by the LEA under Part B below the level of those expenditures for the preceding fiscal year. There have been significant changes to those situations, including:

- Deleting the phrase "who are replaced by qualified lower-salaried staff" in the exception that states "the voluntary departure, by retirement or otherwise, or departure for just cause, of special education or related service personnel";

- Deleting provisions related to conformity with school board policies, collective bargaining agreements, and state statutes, in addressing retirements or resignations and replacements; and

- Adding an exception for the "assumption of cost by the high cost fund." In the Comments and Analysis section, the Department further clarifies that the creation of a "high cost fund" is new in IDEA 2004 and permits states to establish a fund to pay for some high costs associated with certain children with disabilities. The establishment of this fund by the state could "logically and appropriately result in lower expenditures for some LEAs."

Q

How do the regulations address the relationship between reducing maintenance of effort and using Part B funds for early intervening services?

A

The regulations state that up to 15% of IDEA Part B funds can be used to develop and implement early intervening services. The amount of funds spent by an LEA for early intervening services counts toward the maximum amount of expenditures that the LEA may reduce under the adjustment to local fiscal efforts.

The regulations explain the relationship between reducing maintenance of effort and using Part B funds for early intervening services by stating in Appendix D to Part 300, "LEAs that seek to reduce their local maintenance of effort...and use some of their Part B funds for early intervening services...must do so with caution because the local maintenance of effort reduction provision and the authority to use Part B funds for early intervening services are interconnected. The decisions that an LEA makes about the amount of funds that it uses for one purpose affect the amount that it may use for the other."

Q

What changes have been made to clarify an LEA's permissive use of funds?

A

Revisions regarding the permissive use of Part B funds by LEAs include:

- Removing the provision regarding the development and implementation of an integrated and coordinated services system; and

- Adding provisions for addressing early intervening services, high cost special education, related services, and administrative case management.

Q
A

What new provisions have been added concerning the treatment of charter schools and their students?

Changes that were made in the regulations regarding charter schools include:

- Clarifying providing supplementary and related services on site at charter schools to the same extent as is done at public schools; and

- Providing clarification on the distribution and timing of Part B funds to charter schools by LEAs.

Q
A

What state-level activities are detailed in the regulations?

Two state-level activities are mandatory:

- Monitoring, enforcement, and complaint investigation; and

- Establishing and maintaining a mediation process.

The regulations provide the following list as activities that may be carried out:

- For support and direct services, including technical assistance, personnel preparation, and professional development and training;

- To support paperwork reduction activities including expanding the use of technology in the IEP process;

- To assist LEAs in providing positive behavioral interventions and supports and mental health services for children with disabilities;

- To improve the use of technology in the classroom by children with disabilities to enhance learning;

- To support the use of technology, including technology with universal design principles and assistive technology devices, to maximize accessibility to the general education curriculum for children with disabilities;

- For the development and implementation of transition programs, including coordination of services with agencies involved in supporting the transition of student with disabilities to post-secondary activities;

- To assist LEAs in meeting personnel shortages;

- To support capacity building activities and improve the delivery of services by LEAs to improve the results of children with disabilities;

- For alternative programming for children with disabilities who have been expelled from school; and services for children with disabilities in correctional facilities, children enrolled in state-operated or state-supported schools, and children with disabilities in charter schools;

- To support the development and provision of appropriate accommodations for children with disabilities, or the development and provision of alternate assessments that are valid and reliable for assessing the performance of children with disabilities in accordance with ESEA; and

- To provide technical assistance to schools and LEAs, and direct services, including supplemental education services, as described in ESEA, to children with disabilities, in schools or LEAs identified for improvement under ESEA on the sole basis of the assessment results of the subgroup of children with disabilities, including providing professional development to special and general education teachers who teach children with disabilities based on scientifically based research to improve educational instruction in order to improve academic achievement to meet or exceed the objectives established by the state under ESEA.

Q
A

How do the regulations describe a "high-cost fund"?

A "high-cost fund" is intended to address the needs of high need children with disabilities. A major component of these new procedures is the development of a state plan that must address multiple content requirements. Examples of required components in a state plan include:

- A definition of a high need child with a disability that addresses the financial impact that this child has on the budget of LEA (this cost must be 3 times the average per pupil expenditure);

- Establish criteria for participation by an LEA;

- Establish criteria to ensure that placements supported by the high cost fund meet the LRE requirements;

- Develop a funding mechanism that provides distributions each fiscal year to LEAs that meet the criteria; and

- Establish an annual schedule by which the SEA must make its distribution from the high cost fund.

Q

How is the "high-cost fund" funded?

A

A state has the option to reserve for each fiscal year 10% of the amount of funds the state reserves for other state-level activities to finance the high cost fund and support innovative and effective ways of cost sharing by the state, by an LEA or among a consortium of LEAs. The state may not use this 10%, which is solely for disbursements to LEAs, for costs associated with establishing, supporting, and administering the fund, but may use the funds illustrated under state administration. Further, a state must not use more than 5% of the 10% to support innovative and effective ways of cost sharing amount consortia of LEAs.

Q

How is funding for early intervening services for schools operated by the Bureau of Indian Affairs detailed in the regulations?

A

The Secretary of the Department of the Interior may allow each elementary and secondary school for Indian children operated or funded by the Secretary of the Department of the Interior to use not more than 15% of its Part B funds, in combination with other amounts (which may include amounts other than education funds) to develop and implement coordinated, early intervening services, which may include interagency financing structures for children kindergarten through Grade 12 who have not been identified as needing special education or related services but who need additional academic and behavioral support to succeed in the general education environment.

Q

What new flexibility has been included in the regulations for the use of funds for Part C?

A

Any state eligible to receive a grant under section 619 (addressing children 3-5 years of age) of IDEA may use funds made available under state administration, reallocation of funds, and preschool grants to develop and implement a state policy jointly with the lead agency under Part C (addressing children birth-2 years of age) of IDEA and the SEA to provide early intervention services. These early intervention services must include an educational component that promotes school readiness and incorporates preliteracy language, and numeracy skills, in accordance with Part C to children with disabilities who are eligible for services under the preschool section of Part B and who previously received services under Part C until the children enter, or are eligible under state law to enter, kindergarten or elementary school.

PRESCHOOL GRANTS FOR CHILDREN WITH DISABILITIES

Q *What general changes were made to IDEA 2004 Part B preschool section 619?*

A Since Parts A and B of IDEA 2004 apply to preschool special education, the changes in these parts are applicable to the provision of services under section 619 of Part B. In addition, there were several other changes in section 619 itself including:

• Deleted reference to "outlying areas" under allocation of preschool grants to states.

• Deleted the phrase stating that state administration funds for preschool grants may also be used for the administration of Part C if the state educational agency is the lead agency for the state under Part C.

• Deleted references to use of funds under other state-level activities to develop a state improvement plan under subpart 1 of Part D.

• Added two new uses of funds under other state-level activities as follows:

– To provide early intervention services (which shall include an educational component that promotes school readiness and incorporates preliteracy, language, and numeracy skills) in accordance with Part C to children with disabilities who are eligible for services under this section (619) and who previously received services under Part C until such children enter, or are eligible under state law to enter, kindergarten; or

– At the state's discretion, to continue service coordination or case management for families who receive services under Part C.

Q *How are "Allocations to States" addressed in the regulations?*

A Under the "Allocation to States" portion of the regulations, IDEA 2004 deletes the 1997 language that states, "After reserving funds for studies and evaluations under...the Act," which is consistent with changes made to the IDEA 2004 statute.

Q *Do the regulations allow funds reserved for state activities to be used if they are not used for administration?*

A Yes. Under the regulations, funds not used for administration under state activities can be used to:

- Provide early intervention services for preschoolers with disabilities who are served under new IDEA 2004 section "Flexibility to Serve Children 3 Years of Age Until Entrance Into Elementary School," and

- Continue to provide service coordination to children served under the new section described previously.

Understanding IDEA 2004:
Frequently Asked Questions

PART C
Infants and Toddlers
With Disabilities

PART C   Infants and Toddlers With Disabilities

[NOTE: The U.S. Department of Education had not issued proposed regulations for IDEA Part C by the time this publication had gone go print in March of 2007. CEC will provide updates, input, and analysis for the Part C regulations as the Department of Education issues proposed regulations, allows for public input, and issues final regulations.
The following are frequently asked questions taken from the IDEA 2004 statute.]

PART C FINDINGS

What changes were made to the Part C findings language as a result of reauthorization?

The following changes were made to the findings section in Part C:

- Added the phrase "and to recognize the significant brain development that occurs during a child's first 3 years of life."

- Deleted the phrase "to minimize the likelihood of institutionalization of individuals with disabilities."

- Deleted the phrase "historically underrepresented populations" and replaced it with the phrase "all children" and added the term "infants and toddlers in foster care."

DEFINITION OF EARLY INTERVENTION SERVICES

What is the definition of early intervention services?

The following changes in the definition were made:

- Added the phrase "as identified by the individualized family services plan team" regarding the designing of developmental services to meet the developmental needs of an infant or toddler with a disability.

- Added "and sign language and cued language services" to speech-language pathology and audiology services. Report language accompanying the final bill stated that "Conferees commend the Office of Special Education & Rehabilitative Services for developing updated early intervention materials that set out the full range of options for families with deaf and hard of hearing children who now have the potential to develop age-appropriate language in whatever modality their parents choose. Dramatic improvements in hearing technology, both hearing aids and cochlear implants, provide new opportunities for families who wish to pursue spoken language for their child with hearing loss. These new materials and efforts further the goals of the IDEA that early intervention personnel actively provide comprehensive and bias-free information on the range of language options available to a child with hearing loss, including the benefits of early amplification and/or early implantation of a cochlear implant."

- Changed the term "nutritionists" to "registered dietitians" under list of qualified personnel.

- Added "vision specialists, including ophthalmologists and optometrists" to the list of qualified personnel.

TEACHERS OF THE DEAF

Q

Why are teachers of the deaf not included in the list of qualified personnel under Part C?

A

Although the Senate bill had included an addition of teachers of the deaf to the list of qualified personnel, the House bill did not include this provision. Teachers of the deaf was not included in the final bill. However, the report accompanying the bill said that "Conferees intend that the term special education includes teachers of the deaf. The conferees recognize that with the recent dramatic rise in newborn hearing screening, more infants are being identified with hearing loss early and they need the services of teachers of the deaf who can meet their language and communication needs."

DEFINITION OF INFANT OR TODDLER WITH A DISABILITY

Q

What change was made to the Part C definition of infant or toddler with a disability?

A

IDEA 2004 adds a new provision describing children that may be served under Part C at a state's discretion as follows: children with disabilities who are eligible for services under section 619 and who previously received services under Part C until such children enter, or are eligible under state law to enter, kindergarten or elementary school, as appropriate, provided that any programs under this part serving such children shall include:

- An educational component that promotes school readiness and incorporates preliteracy, language, and numeracy skills; and

- A written notification to parents of their rights and responsibilities in determining whether their child will continue to receive services under this part of Part C or participate in preschool programs under section 619.

ASSURANCES STATEMENT REGARDING ELIGIBILITY FOR PART C GRANT

Q

What changes were made to the assurances statement regarding eligibility for a Part C grant?

A

Two changes were made as a result of the reauthorization as follows:

- Changed the requirement for states to demonstrate to the Secretary that the state has adopted the policy that early intervention services are available to all infants and toddlers.

- Added to the statewide policy that appropriate early intervention services are available to the following children: infants and toddlers with disabilities who are homeless children and their families, and infants and toddlers with disabilities who are wards of the state.

DEFINITION OF DEVELOPMENTAL DELAY AS A COMPONENT OF STATEWIDE SYSTEM

Q

How is the definition of developmental delay, as a component of the statewide system under Part C, addressed?

A

This provision now reads as follows: "A rigorous definition of the term 'developmental delay' that will be used by the state in carrying out programs under [Part C] in order to appropriately identify infants and toddlers with disabilities that are in need of services under Part C. The report language regarding these changes stated that the Conferees intend that states establish rigorous standards for identifying and serving infants and toddlers with developmental delays. The Conferees believe that these standards should encompass a sufficient scope of developmental delays to ensure that these infants and toddlers receive the benefit of Part C services designed to lessen the infant or toddler's need for future or more extensive services."

AVAILABILITY OF APPROPRIATE EARLY INTERVENTION SERVICES FOR INFANTS AND TODDLERS WITH DISABILITIES

Q

What is the new provision on the state policy for ensuring that appropriate early intervention services are available to infants and toddlers with disabilities and their families?

A

This provision now says that a state policy that is in effect and that ensures that appropriate early intervention services based on scientifically based research, to the extent practicable, are available to all infants and toddlers with disabilities and their families, including Indian infants and toddlers with disabilities and their families residing on a reservation geographically located in the state and infants and toddlers with disabilities who are homeless children and their families.

Q

STATEWIDE SYSTEM COMPONENT REGARDING CHILD FIND

Does the new law change the statewide system component regarding child find under Part C?

A

Yes. The new provision now includes a comprehensive child find system, consistent with Part B, including a system for making referrals to service providers that includes timelines and provides for participation by primary referral sources and that ensures rigorous standards for appropriately identifying infants and toddlers with disabilities for services under Part C that will reduce the need for future services.

Q

PUBLIC AWARENESS COMPONENT OF STATEWIDE SYSTEM

What changes were made to the public awareness component of the statewide system under Part C?

A

The following changes to this requirement were made:

- Added language to include a public awareness program focusing on early identification of infants and toddlers with disabilities, including the preparation and dissemination by the lead agency to all primary referral sources, especially hospitals and physicians, of information to be given to parents, especially to inform parents with premature infants, or infants with other physical risk factors associated with learning or developmental complications, on the availability of early intervention services under Part C and of services under section 619 (preschool), and procedures for assisting such sources in disseminating such information to parents of infants and toddlers with disabilities.

- Report language regarding these changes stated that the Conferees intend that the public awareness program include a broad range of referral sources such as homeless family shelters, clinics and other health service related offices, public schools and officials and staff in the child welfare system.

- Deleted the requirement to have procedures for determining the extent to which such sources described above disseminate such information.

Q

COMPREHENSIVE SYSTEM OF PERSONNEL DEVELOPMENT

What changes were made to the comprehensive system of personnel development (CSPD) component of a statewide system under Part C?

A

The following changes to CSPD were made:

- Deleted reference to Part B CSPD because Part B CSPD has been removed.

- Added new provisions to the component that now states that a comprehensive system of personnel development, including the training of paraprofessionals and the training of primary referral sources with respect to the basic components of early intervention services available in the state that shall (used to be "may") include: (a) implementing innovative strategies and activities for the recruitment and retention of early education service providers; (b) promoting the preparation of early intervention providers who are fully and appropriately qualified to provide early intervention services under this part (Part C); and (c) training personnel to coordinate transition services for infants and toddlers served under Part C from a program providing early intervention services under this part and under Part B (other than section 619), to a preschool program receiving funds under section 619, or another appropriate program; and may include: (i) training personnel to work in rural and inner-city areas; and (ii) training personnel in the emotional and social development of young children.

PERSONNEL QUALIFICATIONS REQUIREMENT

What are the new requirements regarding personnel qualifications under Part C?

The following changes were made:

- Replaced the term "standards" in relationship to personnel requirements with the term "qualifications."

- Deleted the language saying that to the extent such standards are not based on the highest requirements in the state applicable to a specific profession or discipline, the steps the state is taking to require the retraining or hiring of personnel that meet appropriate professional requirements in the state.

- Deleted the phrase "consistent with state law, within 3 years" at the end of the policy statement on personnel qualifications that now says that a state may adopt a policy that includes making ongoing good-faith efforts to recruit and hire appropriately and adequately trained personnel to provide early intervention services to infants and toddlers with disabilities, including, in a geographic area of the state where there is a shortage of such personnel, the most qualified individuals available who are making satisfactory progress toward completing applicable course work necessary to meet the state's standards.

NATURAL ENVIRONMENTS

Q

What changes were made to the natural environments requirement under Part C?

A

Several phrases were added. The requirement now states that, consistent with IFSP requirements:

- To the maximum extent appropriate, early intervention services are provided in natural environments; and

- The provision of early intervention services for any infant or toddler with a disability occurs in a setting other than a natural environment that is most appropriate, as determined by the parent and the individualized family services plan team, only when early intervention cannot be achieved satisfactorily for the infant or toddler in a natural environment.

Report language regarding this provision stated that, "legislation amends current law to recognize that there may be instances when a child's individualized family services plan cannot be implemented satisfactorily in the natural environment. The Conferees intend that in these instances, the child's parents and the other members of the individualized family services plan team will together make this determination and then identify the most appropriate setting in which early intervention services can be provided."

NEW STATE OPTION

Q

What is the new state option under Part C regarding the flexibility to serve children 3 years of age until entrance into elementary school?

A

In general, this new option states that a statewide system may include a state policy, developed and implemented jointly by the lead agency and the SEA, under which parents of children with disabilities who are eligible for services under section 619 (preschool) and previously received services under Part C, may choose the continuation of early intervention services (which shall include an educational component that promotes school readiness and incorporates preliteracy, language, and numeracy skills) for such children under Part C until such children enter, or are eligible under state law to enter, kindergarten.

Q

What are the statewide system requirements for implementing the new state option under Part C regarding the flexibility to serve children 3 years of age until entrance into elementary school?

A

If a state elects to implement this new provision, the statewide system must ensure that:

- Parents of children with disabilities served pursuant to this option are provided annual notice that contains:

> – A description of the rights of such parents to elect to receive services pursuant to this option or under Part B; and
>
> – An explanation of the differences between services provided pursuant to this option and services provided under part B, including:
>
>   ◆ Types of services and the locations at which the services are provided;
>
>   ◆ Applicable procedural safeguards; and
>
>   ◆ Possible costs (including any fees to be charged to families as described in Part C), if any, to parents of infants and toddlers with disabilities.

- Services provided pursuant to this option include an educational component that promotes school readiness and incorporates preliteracy, language, and numeracy skills.

- The state policy will not affect the right of any child served pursuant to this option to instead receive a free appropriate public education under Part B.

- All early intervention services outlined in the child's individualized family services plan under Part C are continued while any eligibility determination is being made for services under this option.

- The parents of infants or toddlers with disabilities as defined by the state provide informed written consent to the state, before such infants or toddlers reach 3 years of age, as to whether such parents intend to choose the continuation of early intervention services pursuant to this option for such infants or toddlers.

- The requirements under transition shall not apply with respect to a child who is receiving services in accordance with this option until not less than 90 days (and at the discretion of the parties to the conference, not more than 9 months) before the time the child will no longer receive those services.

- There will be a referral for evaluation for early intervention services of a child who experiences a substantiated case of trauma due to exposure to family violence (as defined in section 320 of the Family Violence Prevention and Services Act).

Q

What is the reporting requirement if a state elects to implement the new option under Part C regarding the flexibility to serve children 3 years of age until entrance into elementary school?

A

Required information is addressed in the following provision: "If a statewide system includes a state policy, the state shall submit to the Secretary, in the state's report under [Part C], a report on the number and percentage of children with disabilities who are eligible for services under section 619 [preschool] but whose parents choose for such children to continue to receive early intervention services under [Part C]."

Q

What information must be provided on the use of funds if a state elects to implement the new option under Part C regarding the flexibility to serve children 3 years of age until entrance into elementary school?

A

Required information is addressed in the following provision: "If a statewide system includes a state policy described under this option, the policy shall describe the funds (including an identification as federal, state, or local funds) that will be used to ensure that the option described is available to eligible children and families who provide the required consent including fees (if any) to be charged to families under Part C."

Q

What is the impact on a state that elects to implement the new option under Part C regarding the flexibility to serve children 3 years of age until entrance into elementary school relative to the provision of FAPE under Part B?

A

Two new "rules of construction" under Part C addressed this issue. They are:

- If a statewide system includes a state policy regarding this new option, a state that provides services in accordance with this option to a child with a disability who is eligible for services under section 619 (preschool) shall not be required to provide the child with a free appropriate public education under Part B for the period of time in which the child is receiving services under Part C.

- Nothing under this new option shall be construed to require a provider of services under Part C to provide a child served under Part C with a free appropriate public education.

INDIVIDUALIZED FAMILY SERVICES PLANS

Q

What change was made to the general provision that each infant or toddler with a disability and their family receive a written IFSP developed by a multidisciplinary team, including the parents and implemented with parental consent?

A

The above general provision was retained and a phrase was added that included a description of the appropriate transition services for the infant or toddler.

Q

What changes were made to the content of the IFSP?

A

There were multiple changes to the content of the IFSP as follows:

• Deleted the term major as a modifier for outcomes and added language stating that a statement of the measurable results or outcomes expected to be achieved for the infant or toddler and the family, including preliteracy and language skills, as developmentally appropriate for the child, and the criteria, procedures, and timelines used to determine the degree to which progress toward achieving the results or outcomes is being made and whether modifications or revisions of the results or outcomes or services are necessary.

• Added language to a statement of specific early intervention services based on peer-reviewed research, to the extent practicable, necessary to meet the unique needs of the infant or toddler and the family, including the frequency, intensity, and method of delivering services.

• Added the projected dates for initiation of services and the anticipated length, duration and frequency of the services.

• Added the identification of the service coordinator from the profession most immediately relevant to the infant's or toddler's or family's needs (or who is otherwise qualified to carry out all applicable responsibilities under this part) who will be responsible for the implementation of the plan and coordination with other agencies and persons, including transition services.

PARENTAL CONSENT

Q

How did the provision regarding parental consent change under Part C?

A

The word "only" was added. This provision now states that the contents of the individualized family services plan shall be fully explained to the parents and informed written consent from the parents shall be obtained prior to the provision of early intervention services described in such plan. If the parents do not provide consent with respect to a particular early intervention service, then only the early intervention services to which consent is obtained shall be provided.

STATE APPLICATION FOR PART C FUNDS

What changes were made to the content of the state application for Part C funds regarding financial responsibility?

Two changes were made as follows:

- Deleted language requiring the designation of an individual or entity responsible for assigning financial responsibility among appropriate agencies.

- Replaced the previous provision with a certification to the Secretary that the arrangements to establish financial responsibility for services provided under Part C pursuant to the section regarding payor of last resort, including obligations related to and methods of ensuring services, (i.e., interagency agreements), are current as of the date of submission of the certification.

How was the content of the state application for Part C funds regarding referral for early intervention services changed?

A description of the state policies and procedures was added that require the referral for early intervention services under Part C of a child under the age of 3 who:

- Is involved in a substantiated case of child abuse or neglect; or

- Is identified as affected by illegal substance abuse, or withdrawal symptoms resulting from prenatal drug exposure.

  Report language regarding this new provision stated that "Conferees intend that every child described above will be screened by a Part C provider or designated primary referral source to determine whether a referral for an evaluation for early intervention services under Part C is warranted. If the screening indicates the need for a referral, the Conferees expect a referral to be made. However, the Conferees do not intend this provision to require every child described above to receive an evaluation or early intervention services under Part C."

How was the content of the state application for Part C funds regarding transition changed?

Several changes in the required description of policies and procedures for transition were made as follows:

- Added references to children receiving services under the new state option to serve children 3 years of age until entrance into elementary school and those exiting the program.

- Changed up to 6 months to not more than 9 months in the language related to timelines for convening the transition conference for children who may be eligible for Part B preschool services.

- Added language to the existing requirement to establish a transition plan, including, as appropriate, steps to exit from the program.

Does the content of the state application for Part C address collaboration with other programs?

Yes. A new provision was added that required a description of state efforts to promote collaboration among Early Head Start programs under section 645A of the Head Start Act, early education and child care programs, and services under Part C.

Were any additions made to the assurance statement on the involvement of underserved groups in the state application for Part C funds?

Yes. Homeless children and children with disabilities who are wards of the state were added to the list of underserved groups.

OPTIONAL USE OF PART C FUNDS

Did the optional use of Part C funds change?

Yes. A new provision was added regarding how a state may use its Part C funds as follows: With the written consent of the parents, to continue to provide early intervention services under Part C to children with disabilities from their third birthday until such children enter, or are eligible under state law to enter, kindergarten, in lieu of a FAPE provided in accordance with Part B.

PAYOR OF LAST RESORT

How does IDEA 2004 address the payor of last resort provision under Part C?

An extensive set of procedures was added regarding obligations related to and methods of ensuring services as follows: The new law states that the Chief Executive Officer of a State or designee of the officer shall ensure that an interagency agreement or other mechanism for interagency coordination is in effect between each public agency and the designated lead agency, in order to ensure:

- The provision of, and financial responsibility for, services provided under this part; and

- Such services are consistent with the requirements of section 635 and the State's application pursuant to section 637, including the provision of such services during the pendency of any such dispute.

The law also states that if a public agency other than an educational agency fails to provide or pay for the services under an agreement required under paragraph (1) above, the Chief Executive Officer can order the local educational agency or state agency to provide or pay for the provision of services to the child.

The LEA or SEA is then authorized to claim reimbursement for the services from the public agency that failed to provide or pay for the services and the public agency must reimburse the local educational agency or state agency according to the terms of the interagency agreement or other mechanism required under paragraph (1) above.

The requirements of paragraph (1) above can be met by:

- State statute or regulation;

- Signed agreements between agency officials that clearly identify the responsibilities of each agency relating to the provision of services; or

- Other appropriate written methods as determined by the Chief Executive Officer of the state or designee of the officer and approved by the Secretary of Education.

STATE INTERAGENCY COORDINATING COUNCIL

Was the provision for the State Interagency Coordinating Council (SICC) changed?

Yes. The following changes were made to the SICC requirements:

- Added new required members to the SICC including representatives from: the state Medicaid agency, the Office of the Coordinator of Education of Homeless Children and Youth, the state child welfare agency responsible for foster care, and the state agency responsible for children's mental health.

- The term governance was changed to regulation in relation to the agency responsible for the state regulation of health insurance.

- Changed the conflict of interest language as follows: No member of the council shall cast a vote on any matter that is likely to provide a direct financial benefit to that member or otherwise give the appearance of a conflict of interest under state law. The language would provide was deleted.

Q
A

ALLOCATION OF FUNDS

How was allocation of funds provisions under Part C addressed?

New provisions were added for funding the optional state program regarding flexibility to serve children 3 years of age until entrance into elementary school. The new law states that if at any time appropriations for the Part C program exceed $460 million, then the Secretary of Education is required to reserve 15% of the appropriations for state incentive grants to states that are implementing extended Part C services.

Grants will be made to states in an amount that bears the same ratio to the amount reserved under such paragraph as the number of infants and toddlers in all states receiving grants. A state that receives a grant under this section of the law cannot receive an amount greater than 20% of the total amount reserved in any fiscal year.

If grant amounts are not obligated and spent prior to the beginning of the firs fiscal year for which they were appropriated, those amounts remain available for obligation and expenditure for the first succeeding fiscal year. Any amounts that are not obligated and spent prior to the beginning of the second fiscal year that comes after the first succeeding fiscal year must be returned to the Department of Education.

Q
A

FEDERAL INTERAGENCY COORDINATING COUNCIL

What is the status of the Federal Interagency Coordinating Council (FICC)?

Reference to the FICC was deleted in the new law.

Q
A

AUTHORIZATION OF APPROPRIATIONS

What changes were made to the section on authorization of appropriations under Part C?

This section was renumbered and is now section 644. Part C has been authorized at such sums as may be necessary for each year from 2005 to 2010. Part C was not permanently authorized.

Understanding IDEA 2004:
Frequently Asked Questions

PART D

National Activities to Improve Education of Children With Disabilities

PART D National Activities to Improve Education of Children With Disabilities

Q *What are the overall changes in Part D?*

A The Individuals With Disabilities Education Improvement Act of 2004 made a number of significant substantive, organizational, and administrative changes in the Part D National Activities to Improve Education of Children With Disabilities. The programs authorized historically by IDEA and, in some cases, in earlier federal legislation, have provided the critical infrastructure in such areas as research, professional development, technical assistance, technology and media services, and dissemination of information that has supported SEAs and LEAs to improve services and outcomes for children with disabilities.

Part D has been given a new structure in the statute. Formerly organized into two subparts, Part D now has four subparts. Those former and current subparts and the authorities under each are depicted in the following chart and then discussed in questions and answers about Part D and changes in its programs.

PART D - IDEA 1997	PART D - IDEA 2004
Subpart 1: State Program Improvement Grants	**Subpart 1:** State Personnel Development Grants
Subpart 2: Coordinated Research, Personnel Preparation, Technical Assistance, Support, and Dissemination of Information	**Subpart 2:** Personnel Preparation, Technical Assistance, Model Demonstration Projects, and Dissemination of Information
Chapter 1	• Personnel development to improve services and results for children with disabilities
• Administrative provisions	• Technical assistance, demonstration projects, dissemination of information, and implementation of scientifically based research
• Research and innovation to improve services and results for children with disabilities	• Studies and evaluations
• Personnel preparation to improve services and results for children with disabilities	• Interim alternative educational settings, behavioral supports, and systemic school interventions
• Studies and evaluations	**Subpart 3:** Supports to Improve Results for Children With Disabilities
Chapter 2	• Parent training and information centers
• Parent training and information centers	• Community parent resource centers
• Community parent resource centers	• Technical assistance for parent training and information centers
• Technical assistance for parent training and information centers	• Technology development, demonstration, and utilization; media services; and instructional materials
• Coordinated technical assistance and dissemination	**Subpart 4:** General Provisions
• Technology development, demonstration, and utilization, and media services	

The most significant change in Part D is that the program of research and innovation for children with disabilities has been removed from the statute, and a new research authority addressing the needs of children with disabilities has been placed in the federal Education Sciences Reform Act. In addition, the responsibility for the administration of research in the education of children with disabilities has been moved from the Office of Special Education Programs to the research unit of the U.S. Department of Education, the Institute of Education Sciences. Because the research program is no longer authorized in Part D, it is discussed separately at the end of the following Part D discussion.

Q

Has the U.S. Department of Education published regulations for the Part D programs?

A

The Department published final regulations on June 5, 2006 that address the Service Obligation requirements of students who receive financial assistance from IDEA personnel preparation grants. Regulations covering the other Part D authorities have not been published and are not expected. Instead, the controlling authority for virtually all Part D activities is what is in the IDEA Amendments of 2004.

STATE PERSONNEL DEVELOPMENT GRANTS

Q

What are the overall changes to the State Personnel Development Grants Program?

A

The State Personnel Development Grants Program replaces the State Improvement Grant (SIG) Program that was added to IDEA with the enactment of the 1997 Amendments. Although the purpose of the former program focused on improving state systems for providing educational, early intervention, and transitional services through personnel development, technical assistance, and dissemination activities, this new program of grants to states focuses exclusively on personnel.

Q

What is the purpose of the State Personnel Development Grant Program?

A

The purpose of the State Personnel Development Program is to improve State systems for personnel preparation and personnel development in early intervention, educational, and transition services in order to improve results for children with disabilities.

Q

Does the new program, like its predecessor, require states to form a partnership with other entities in order to receive a grant?

A

Yes, although grants are awarded to SEAs, in order to be eligible for funding, an SEA must form a partnership. This partnership must include LEAs, at least one institution of higher education, State agencies responsible for administering Part C, early education, child care, vocational rehabilitation programs, and the entity responsible for teacher preparation and certification if that entity is not the SEA. Other partners are to be selected by the SEA from those identified in the law.

Q

A

What kind of planning is required of the partnership?

The SEA application must include a state plan that identifies and addresses State and local needs for personnel preparation and professional development of personnel serving infants, toddlers, preschoolers and children with disabilities. This plan must be based on an assessment of needs and describe activities to be conducted as well as the roles and responsibilities of each member of the partnership. The plan is to be integrated and aligned with state plans and activities under ESEA, the Rehabilitation Act, and the Higher Education Act. To carry out its plan, an SEA must award subgrants or contracts to LEAs, IHEs, parent training and information centers or community parent resource centers, as appropriate.

Q

A

What types of activities may states carry out under this program?

SEA partnerships will have considerable discretion in identifying and designing activities to meet the personnel needs outlined in their state plan. At least 90% of grant funds must be spent on professional development activities to improve the knowledge, skills, and effectiveness of personnel serving children with disabilities, and may include general educators in their activities. Not more than 10% of grant funds may be used to support other activities that primarily address policy and systemic issues at the state and local level associated with the certification, preparation, recruitment, retention, and ongoing professional development of personnel serving children with disabilities.

Q

A

How will these grants be financed and how much money was authorized?

Grant awards are to range from $500,000 to $4 million a year for States and be at least $80,000 a year for outlying areas. A State which currently has a SIG grant may elect to continue that grant until it expires, or may instead opt to apply for a grant under the new program. Awards of up to 5 years each will be made on a competitive basis until such time as the funds available exceed $100,000,000/ year. When available funds exceed that figure, grants from that point on will be awarded on the same formula basis that applies to Part B funds allocated to States under Sec 611(d). The law authorizes Congress to appropriate such sums as may be necessary for this program in each year through FY 2010. Congress appropriated $50.7 million for the program for FY2005, $50.1 million for FY2006, and $50.7 million for FY2007.

PERSONNEL PREPARATION, TECHNICAL ASSISTANCE, MODEL DEMONSTRATION PROJECTS, AND DISSEMINATION OF INFORMATION

Q

What are the purposes of the Personnel Preparation, Technical Assistance, Model Demonstration Projects, and Dissemination of Information Program?

A

According to IDEA 2004, the purposes of Subpart 2 are:

- To provide federal funding for personnel preparation, technical assistance, model demonstration projects, information dissemination, and studies and evaluations, in order to improve early intervention, educational, and transitional results for children with disabilities; and

- To assist SEAs and LEAs in improving their education systems for children with disabilities.

PERSONNEL PREPARATION TO IMPROVE SERVICES AND RESULTS FOR CHILDREN WITH DISABILITIES

Q

What is the aim of the Personnel Preparation to Improve Services and Results for Children With Disabilities Program?

A

Under this authority, the federal government provides financial assistance to increase the number and quality of personnel serving children with disabilities. A major activity supported by this program is preservice training of special education teachers, early intervention providers and related services personnel, including personnel who are underrepresented in the field. In addition, this program helps to finance training at the doctoral level of leadership personnel such as special education administrators, researchers, and personnel preparation faculty in universities.

Q

What activities can be supported under this program?

A

The personnel development program authorizes competitive grants, contracts and cooperative agreements for activities to improve services and results for all children with disabilities, birth through age 21, consistent with State-identified needs. Building on a long-standing IDEA program to increase the number of qualified personnel serving children with both high- and low-incidence disabilities, the revised program emphasizes several areas of focus for future funding, including:

- Addressing student conduct and improving results in academics and core content areas;

- Incorporating the use of scientifically based research into training activities: Supporting paraprofessionals, administrators, and beginning special educators; and

- Helping special and general educators working in collaboration to improve results for children with disabilities.

The law continues to highlight the need to reduce personnel shortages by requiring that support be provided for the preparation of personnel who will serve children with low-incidence disabilities and personnel serving in leadership positions in early intervention, school programs, research, and personnel training.

Q

A

What new activities will the Personnel Development program support?

The law authorizes a new initiative aimed at improving the effectiveness of personnel at the beginning of their careers. It requires that the Secretary award funds for Enhanced Support for Beginning Special Educators. Grants are to be awarded for such activities as incorporating into preservice training programs an extended clinical learning opportunity, field experience or supervised practicum, and creating or supporting teacher-faculty partnerships (such as professional development schools). These teacher-faculty partnerships must include at least one institution of higher education and at least one LEA that serves a high proportion of low-income students or at least one elementary or secondary school that has failed to make annual yearly progress, as required by ESEA, based on the assessment results of students with disabilities. In addition, these partnerships may include other entities, and may provide mentoring and induction opportunities with ongoing support for beginning teachers.

Q

A

How does IDEA 2004 affect the Service Obligation requirements under the Personnel Preparation Program?

Historically, most IDEA grants for the preservice preparation of personnel to serve children with disabilities have included substantial funding for student scholarships, as a means of recruiting people into the special education, early intervention, and related encouraging fields. Beginning with the 1997 Amendments, IDEA required that individuals who receive a scholarship from these grants agree to work after completing their program for a period of 2 years in the field for every year for which they received scholarship support, or repay the federal government for the scholarship assistance they received. The responsibility for tracking student compliance with the work requirement was placed on grantees–the institutions of higher education that receive the IDEA training grants and allocate financial assistance to students preparing for work in special education, related services, early intervention, and leadership positions.

IDEA 2004 reaffirmed the requirement that students who receive scholarship support from an IDEA training grant work for a period of 2 years in the field for every year for which they received scholarship support, or repay the federal government for the assistance they received. The statute made two changes of note in:

- Requiring that the Secretary, rather than the grantee, track the employment of scholarship recipients in order to ensure that students fulfill their service obligation and, further, authorizing the Secretary to use 0.5% of the funds appropriated for personnel preparation activities to carry out this compliance responsibility; and

- Permitting the Secretary to reduce or waive the service obligation requirement if the Secretary determines that it is acting as a deterrent to recruiting students into special education or a related field.

Q
A

Do the Service Obligation regulations make any changes in how the requirements are implemented?

Yes, on June 5, 2006 the Department issued final regulations that apply to personnel preparation grants awarded after July 5, 2006 and the students who receive scholarships from those grants (grants awarded before July 5, 2006 are subject to earlier regulations published December 9, 1999). The 2006 regulations were developed (a) to reflect changes in the Service Obligation requirements authorized by the IDEA Amendments of 2004, and (b) to remedy some problems with and clarify selected provisions of the previous regulations. Regulatory changes of significance are:

- Definition of "Eligible Employment." IDEA 2004 regulations clarify the types of work that satisfy the service obligation. Students may satisfy their service obligation by working as providers of special education, related services or early intervention services for children with disabilities, or in a wide variety of positions "related to the training for which the scholarship was received." These regulations clarify that all students, including those who receive IDEA scholarship support for study in undergraduate, master's or licensure programs (like their counterparts in doctoral training programs) can satisfy their obligation not only through working directly with children with disabilities but also through jobs "related to the training for which the scholarship was received." The regulations specifically identify such jobs as supervision, teaching at the postsecondary level, research, policy, technical assistance, program development, and administration as eligible types of employment.

In addition, the 2006 regulations also clarify that individuals who satisfy their obligation by working directly with children with disabilities must work in a position in which at least 51% of the infants, toddlers, and children they serve are receiving special education, related services, or early intervention services from the student, or the student spends 51% of his or her time providing those services to children with disabilities. Similarly, individuals who satisfy their obligation through other forms of eligible employment (e.g., research, university teaching, administration, etc.) must spend 51% of their time performing work related to the training for which a scholarship was received.

- Grace Period. All students will have a 5-year grace period (an increase from 3 years in earlier regulations) for completing their obligation. For example, a student who exits with a 2-year obligation is required to satisfy the obligation within 7 years of exit (i.e., 2-year obligation plus 5 years of grace). This extended period is intended to aid those students (e.g., in early intervention) who face more obstacles in finding full-time positions in which they can meet the requirement that 51% of the children they serve or 51% of their work time is spent providing special education, related services, or early intervention services to children with disabilities.

- Student Employment Tracking. At the completion of a student's program:

  - The grantee must inform and secure written agreement from a student on the amount of financial assistance the student was provided by the grant, the length of time the student must work in order to satisfy the obligation, the deadline for satisfying the obligation, and procedures the student must follow until the obligation is satisfied.

  - The grantee must transfer to the U.S. Department of Education information the Department needs in order to track a student's progress in meeting their service obligation after program completion (e.g., identity, length of the service obligation, deadline for satisfying it).

  - Within 60 days after exiting the training program and thereafter, as necessary, the student must provide the Department all information the Secretary needs to monitor the student's progress to satisfy the service obligation, including social security number, address, employment setting, and employment status.

- Exceptions and Deferrals. Under the 1999 regulations, grantees were responsible for granting student requests for exceptions and deferrals of the service obligation. IDEA 2004 removes this responsibility from grantees and place it, instead, with the U.S. Department of Education.

Q

How much money did Congress authorize for these personnel preparation activities?

A

IDEA 2004 authorized Congress to appropriate such sums as may be necessary for activities carried out under the personnel preparation program for each of the fiscal years 2005 through 2010. For FY 2005, Congress appropriated $90.6 million; for FY 2006 and FY 2007 Congress appropriated $89.7 million in each year for this program.

TECHNICAL ASSISTANCE, DEMONSTRATION PROJECTS, DISSEMINATION OF INFORMATION, AND IMPLEMENTATION OF SCIENTIFICALLY BASED RESEARCH

Q

What were the overall changes to Technical Assistance, Demonstration Projects, Dissemination of Information, and Implementation of Scientifically Based Research?

A

This section of Subpart 2 represents a significant revision of what was previously the Part D authority for Coordinated Technical Assistance and Dissemination. It revises the former program and both requires the Secretary to conduct initiatives in new areas and permits the Secretary to conduct activities in other areas identified in the statute. New priority is placed on activities that promote the academic achievement of children with disabilities and that improve the effectiveness of assessments to determine adequate yearly progress under the ESEA. In addition, this section authorizes the Secretary to conduct demonstration and outreach/implementation activities that were previously authorized under the Part D research program.

Due to the extent of changes in this section, the information below highlights the required and permissible activities designated in the law.

Q

What technical assistance, demonstration, dissemination and research implementation activities is the Secretary required to conduct under this section?

A

The Secretary is required to support activities to improve services provided under IDEA that promote academic achievement and improve results for children with disabilities. These activities may address the practice of professionals and others involved in providing services to children with disabilities. Among the activities authorized under this section, the following are required:

• Implementing effective strategies for addressing inappropriate behavior of students with disabilities in schools, including strategies for preventing children with emotional and behavioral problems from developing problems so severe that they require the provision of special education and related services;

- Improving the alignment, compatibility, and development of valid and reliable assessments and alternative assessments for determining adequate yearly progress under the ESEA;

- Providing training for both general and special education teachers to address the needs of students with different learning styles;

- Disseminating information about effective curricula designs, instructional approaches, and strategies; identifying positive academic and social learning opportunities in order to provide effective transitions between educational settings or from school to postschool settings; and improving educational and transitional results with an emphasis on improving the progress of children with disabilities as measured by assessments within the general education curriculum; and

- Applying scientifically based findings to facilitate system changes in policy, procedure, practice, and the training and use of personnel related to the education of children with disabilities.

What activities is the Secretary permitted, but not required, to carry out under this revised authority?

At the discretion of the Secretary, other activities may be carried out to achieve the same purposes, as stated previously for required activities. Those activities are to improve services provided under IDEA that promote academic achievement and improve results for children with disabilities. Among the authorized activities are:

- Applying and testing research findings to determine the usefulness, effectiveness, and applicability of research findings in areas such as improving instructional methods, curricula, and tools;

- Supporting coordination of early intervention and educational services with services provided by health, rehabilitation, and social service agencies;

- Promoting alignment and compatibility of general and special education reforms;

- Assisting parents, professionals, and other persons to learn about and implement scientifically based research findings and successful practices for serving children with disabilities;

- Conducting outreach and dissemination activities for personnel serving children with disabilities related to successful approaches to overcoming systemic barriers to effective and efficient delivery of early intervention, educational, and transitional services;

- Assisting SEAs and LEAs to plan systemic changes for improving services, and promoting changes on a multistate or regional basis to assist States, school districts, and others in partnerships that are attempting to achieve systemic-change outcomes;

- Addressing the needs and issues specific to populations of children with disabilities through technical assistance and inservice training, such as children who are deaf-blind, who are deaf or hard-of-hearing, who have autism spectrum disorders, or have other low-incidence disabilities;

- Demonstrating models of personnel preparation to ensure appropriate placements and services for all students with disabilities, and to reduce disproportionality in eligibility, placement, and disciplinary actions for minority and limited English proficient children with disabilities; and

- Disseminating information on how to reduce inappropriate racial and ethnic disproportionalities identified through State data reporting under Sec. 618.

Q

Do any special requirements apply to grants, cooperative agreements, and contracts awarded under this program?

A

Yes, IDEA 2004 places several specific requirements on applications for funding and on activities carried out under this program:

- The Secretary must ensure there is an appropriate balance across all age ranges of children with disabilities in carrying out this section;

- The Secretary is required to support projects that link States to technical assistance resources and to make research and related products available through libraries, electronic networks, parent training projects, and other information sources;

- To the extent feasible, an applicant for funding must demonstrate that the project they propose conducting is supported by scientifically valid research that has been carried out in accordance with the standards for the conduct and evaluation of research and development established by the National Center for Education Research; and

- As appropriate, the Secretary is to give priority to applications that propose to serve teachers and school personnel directly in school settings.

STUDIES AND EVALUATIONS

Q

What are the overall changes to the Studies and Evaluations Program?

A

IDEA 2004 continues to authorize activities to assess the implementation of IDEA and its effectiveness in meeting the needs of children with disabilities, including two major and highly visible activities, the national assessment and the annual report to Congress. Several significant changes in this authority as well as a number of technical and minor changes have been made.

Q
A

What new activities are authorized under the Studies and Evaluations Program?

Studies in two new areas have been authorized by the amendments, one concerning students who take alternate assessments and the other concerning a new provision in the Part C early intervention program.

In the first, one or more studies are to be conducted to address accountability for students who are held to alternative achievement standards. Congress authorizes the Secretary to reserve $1 million in FY 2005 to finance this study, and additional funds in subsequent years if necessary. These studies are to examine:

• The criteria that States use to determine eligibility for alternate assessments and the number and type of children who take those assessments and who are held accountable to alternative achievement standards;

• The validity and reliability of alternate assessment instruments and procedures;

• The alignment of alternate assessments and achievement standards to State academic content standards in reading, math, and science; and

• The use and effectiveness of alternate assessments in appropriately measuring student progress and outcomes specific to individualized instructional need.

The second new activity calls for a study and report to Congress on the extent to which States exercise the new option provided under Part C to adopt policies that permit parents of children receiving Part C early intervention services to extend those services until they are eligible to enter kindergarten and on the effect of those policies.

Q
A

Has the main focus of the National Assessment changed?

Although the purpose of the National Assessment remains the same (i.e., to determine the effectiveness of IDEA in achieving its purposes and to provide information to Congress, States, and other stakeholders on how it might be implemented more effectively), the reauthorization broadens the scope of the assessment by requiring examination in several new areas. The scope has been expanded to include an assessment of:

- The impact of programs supported under IDEA addressing students' developmental needs and improving their academic achievement to enable them to reach challenging developmental goals and State academic content standards based on State academic assessments;

- The types of programs and services that demonstrate the greatest likelihood of helping students reach challenging State academic content standards and developmental goals;

- The implementation of the professional development activities assisted under IDEA and the impact on instruction, student academic achievement, and teacher qualifications to enhance the ability of special and general education teachers to improve results for children with disabilities; and

- The effectiveness of the Secretary, schools, States and other entities that receive assistance under IDEA in achieving the purposes of the Act by (a) improving academic achievement of children with disabilities and their performance on regular statewide assessments (as compared to nondisabled children) and the performance of children with disabilities on alternate assessments; (b) addressing the reading and literacy needs of children with disabilities; and (c) reducing the inappropriate overidentification of children, especially minority and limited English proficient children, as having a disability.

Q

What new data on children from minority backgrounds will be collected as part of the National Assessment?

A

In conducting the assessment, the Secretary is required to include a range of information on children with disabilities from minority backgrounds. To existing requirements for data on minority children, the amendments add requirements for data on the number of minority children who (a) graduate from secondary school with a regular diploma in the standard number of years, and (b) drop out of the educational system.

Q

Have any topics or requirements been dropped from the National Assessment?

A

Yes, the amendments delete from the scope of the National Assessment two topics which addressed:

- Behavioral problems of children with disabilities as compared to nondisabled children; and

- Coordination of services provided under IDEA with each other, with other educational and pupil services, and with health and social services funded from other sources.

In addition, IDEA 2004 no longer requires that the Secretary plan, review, and conduct the National Assessment in consultation with researchers, State and local practitioners, parents, individuals with disabilities, and other appropriate individuals.

Q

When will reports from the National Assessment be available?

A

IDEA 2004 establishes new due dates for both the interim and final reports on the National Assessment. The interim report must be submitted to the President and Congress no later than 3 years after the date of enactment of the IDEA amendments, and the final report submitted no later than 5 years after enactment. Thus, these reports will be due, respectively, by December 2007 and December 2009.

Q

How was the Annual Report affected by IDEA 2004?

A

Two new reporting requirements were added by the statute. The first requires the Secretary to report each year on the extent and progress of the assessment of national activities conducted under Part D programs, and the second directs the Secretary to summarize the research conducted by the new National Center for Special Education Research at IES.

Q

What other changes in the Studies and Evaluations Program have been made?

A

IDEA 2004 eliminates from this program the requirement that the Secretary provide technical assistance to LEAs to assist them in carrying out local capacity-building and improvement projects and other LEA systemic improvement activities.

Q

What administrative changes have been made to the Studies and Evaluations Program?

A

The most significant change for the Studies and Evaluations program is in its administration. Effective upon enactment, the law directs the Secretary to delegate to the Director of the Institute of Education Sciences (IES) the responsibility for carrying out all but two activities authorized under the Studies and Evaluations program. Effective December 2004, the IES Director was assigned responsibility for the National Assessment and for all activities related to its conduct. The Office of Special Education Programs (OSEP) retains responsibility for carrying out the newly authorized study of States' policies under Part C as well as for the preparation of the Annual Report to Congress on the implementation and impact of IDEA. Noticeably absent in this administrative division is any requirement for consultation or collaboration between IES and OSEP in carrying out their respective responsibilities.

Q

Has the set-aside that has financed the Studies and Evaluations Program since 1997 been affected by the reauthorization?

A

Yes, the funding set-aside was eliminated by IDEA 2004. Since 1997 the Department has been authorized to set aside each year 0.5% of funds appropriated for the Parts B and C programs, up to $20 million annually, to carry out the Studies and Evaluations program. In its place, the 2004 amendments authorize Congress to appropriate such sums as necessary to finance activities authorized under Subpart 3, including activities conducted under the Studies and Evaluations Program.

INTERIM ALTERNATIVE EDUCATIONAL SETTINGS, BEHAVIORAL SUPPORTS, AND SYSTEMIC SCHOOL INTERVENTIONS

Q

What is the overall focus for the Interim Alternative Educational Settings, Behavioral Supports, and Systemic School Interventions?

A

This is a new program in IDEA that authorizes funds for activities to provide safe learning environments that support academic achievement for all students by improving the quality of interim alternative educational settings and by providing increased behavioral supports and research-based, systemic interventions in schools.

Q

Who is eligible to receive funding under this program?

A

Eligible applicants for funding are (a) LEAs and (b) consortia which include at least one LEA and other entities such as another LEA, an institution of higher education, a community-based organization with a proven track record in helping children with disabilities who have behavioral challenges, a community mental health provider, or an educational service agency.

Q

What kinds of activities can be carried out in the area of behavioral supports and systemic interventions?

A

Funding may be provided for establishing or expanding the scope of:

- Training of school staff on early identification, prereferral, and referral procedures;

- Training of administrators, teachers, and other school staff in positive behavioral supports and interventions, including joint training of such personnel and parents;

- Developing and implementing curriculum, programs, and interventions; and

- Strengthening linkages between school-based and community-based services.

What types of activities can be supported to improve interim alternative educational settings?

Authorized activities in this area include:

- Improving training of administrators, teachers, related services personnel, behavioral specialists, and other school staff in behavioral supports and interventions;

- Attracting and retaining a high quality, diverse staff;

- Making referrals to counseling services;

- Promoting effective case management and collaboration among parents, school staff, physicians, and others involved with the child; and

- Helping students transition from interim alternative educational settings into their general education classrooms.

How much money will be available to support grants under this program?

Funding for this new program is to be included in the appropriation for Sec. 663, 664, and 665 activities. The decision on how much of that appropriation will be allocated to this program will be made by the U.S. Department of Education.

How much money is authorized for Subpart 2 activities?

IDEA 2004 authorizes Congress to appropriate such sums as may be necessary for each of the fiscal years 2005 to 2010 to carry out all sections under this subpart except Sec. 662 for which a separate authorization of appropriations is provided. The statute authorizes Congress to appropriate such sums as may be necessary for each of the fiscal years 2005 through 2010 for Sec. 662. The effect of this separate authorization for Sec. 662, the Personnel Preparation authority, is that Congress will appropriate funds specifically for Sec. 662. All other Subpart 2 programs will be funded under a separate appropriation and the Secretary of the Department of Education will allocate funds from that amount for each of the remaining Subpart 2 programs.

For FY 2005, Congress appropriated $52.4 million for Subpart 2 activities (not including personnel preparation activities), and $48.9 million for each of the fiscal years 2006 and 2007.

SUPPORT TO IMPROVE RESULTS FOR CHILDREN WITH DISABILITIES

What is the overall purpose of the Supports to Improve Results for Children With Disabilities Program?

The purpose of this part is to ensure that:

- Children with disabilities and their parents receive training and information designed to assist the children in meeting developmental and functional goals and challenging academic achievement goals, and in preparing them to lead productive independent adult lives;

- Children with disabilities and their parents receive training and information on their rights, responsibilities, and protections under this title in order to develop the skills necessary to participate cooperatively and effectively in planning and decision making relating to early intervention, educational, and transitional services;

- Parents, teachers, administrators, early intervention personnel, related services personnel, and transition personnel receive coordinated and accessible technical assistance and information to assist such personnel in improving early intervention, educational, and transitional services and results for children with disabilities and their families; and

- Appropriate technology and media are researched, developed, and demonstrated to improve and implement early intervention, educational, and transitional services, and results for children with disabilities and their families.

PARENT TRAINING AND INFORMATION CENTERS

What is the overall purpose of the Parent Training and Information Centers?

IDEA 2004 continues to authorize financial support for at least one parent training and information center in each state to assist parents in meeting their children's needs and goals, and to participate in planning and decision making related to early intervention, educational, and transitional services. These amendments make some changes in both the governance of centers and in the activities the centers are to carry out.

Q

What changes have been made in the activities that Parent Training and Information Centers (PTIs) will be carrying out?

A

Although most activities that were previously required continue to be required, a few additional activities and topics will need to be addressed by PTIs. These include:

- Providing training and information to parents that assist them in enabling their children with disabilities to meet developmental and functional goals as well as challenging academic achievement goals;

- Ensuring that PTI services meet the needs of low-income parents and parents of limited English proficient children;

- Assisting parents to participate in activities at school that benefit their children;

- Assisting parents in resolving disputes in the most expeditious and effective way, including explaining the benefits and encouraging the use of alternative methods of dispute resolution, including mediation;

- Assisting parents in understanding, preparing for, and participating in resolution sessions, now required in Part B, that take place prior to the conduct of a due process hearing;

- Establishing cooperative partnerships with community parent resources centers; and

- Incorporating into their annual reports to the Secretary of Education data on the number of parents served by the center who have resolved disputes through alternative methods of dispute resolution.

Q

How have the requirements for PTI governance been affected by the new amendments?

A

The mission of an organization which receives a PTI grant must be to serve families of children with disabilities from birth through age 26 who have the full range of disabilities. As a result of this revised mission, IDEA no longer requires that PTIs establish a special governing committee for grant activities. PTIs must have a board of directors the majority of whose members are parents of children with disabilities in the birth through age 26 age range. Parent and professional members of the board must be broadly representative of the population to be served, including low-income parents and parents of limited English proficient children.

COMMUNITY PARENT RESOURCE CENTERS

Q *What is the overall purpose of the Community Parent Resource Centers?*

A IDEA 2004 continues to authorize financial support for local parent organizations to operate community parent resource centers to help ensure that underserved parents of children with disabilities have the training and information they need to enable them to participate effectively in efforts to meet their children's needs. The primary change enacted by the amendments is in the governance of centers.

Q *What governance changes were made by IDEA 2004?*

A IDEA 2004 clarifies that the mission of organizations that receive a grant to support a community parent resource center must be to serve the parents of children with disabilities who are ages birth through 26 and who have the full range of disabilities. These centers are no longer required to establish a special governing committee to administer the federal award.

TECHNICAL ASSISTANCE FOR PARENT TRAINING AND INFORMATION CENTERS

Q *What is the overall purpose of the Technical Assistance for Parent Training and Information Centers?*

A IDEA continues to authorize financial assistance to eligible organizations to provide technical assistance (TA) for developing, assisting, and coordinating parent training and information programs carried out by the PTIs and Community Parent Resource Centers.

Q *Have any changes been made in this TA activity?*

A IDEA 2004 has made minor changes in the technical assistance activities to be carried out under this section. First, the entities funded to provide technical assistance are no longer required to assist PTIs and Community Parent Resource Centers to evaluate themselves. And second, any TA provider funded under this program is required to develop collaborative agreements with the geographically appropriate regional resource center and, as appropriate, with the regional educational laboratory funded by the Institute of Education Sciences in order to further parent and professional collaboration.

TECHNOLOGY DEVELOPMENT, DEMONSTRATION, AND UTILIZATION; MEDIA SERVICES

What are the changes to the Technology Development, Demonstration and Utilization; Media Services?

IDEA 2004 authorized the Secretary to support technology development, demonstration, and utilization activities, as well as instructional media services. IDEA 2004 revises these two authorities and adds a new program that will establish a National Instructional Materials Center to support individuals with print disabilities.

What changes have been made in the Technology Development, Demonstration, and Utilization Program?

IDEA 2004 retains some of the activities previously authorized under this program, while revising or deleting others. Emphasis on universal design has been added. The activities that may now be carried out are:

- Conducting research on and promoting the demonstration and use of innovative, emerging, and universally designed technologies for children with disabilities by improving the transfer of technology from research and development to practice;

- Supporting research, development, and dissemination of technology with universal design features, so that the technology is accessible to the broadest range of individuals without further modification or adaptation;

- Demonstrating the use of systems to provide parents and teachers with information and training concerning early diagnosis of, intervention for, and effective teaching strategies for young children with reading disabilities; and

- Supporting the use of Internet-based communications for students with cognitive disabilities in order to maximize their academic and functional skills.

Activities previously authorized that have been deleted by the 2004 Amendments are:

- Providing technical assistance to recipients of other assistance concerning the development of accessible, effective, and usable products; and

- Communicating information on available technology and the uses of such technology to assist children with disabilities.

Q
A

Have changes been made in the Media Services Program?

Yes, the law now emphasizes that media service activities carried out under this program are to focus on their use in the classroom rather than in a broader array of settings. Of special note is that the 2004 Amendments delete long authorized support for providing cultural experiences to enrich the lives of and promote awareness and understanding of the achievements of children and adults who are deaf and hard of hearing. The educational media activities now authorized under this program are those that:

- Are designed to be of educational value in classroom settings for children with disabilities;

- When not previously provided by the producer or distributor or not fully funded by other sources, provide video description, open captioning, or closed captioning, appropriate for use in the classroom setting, of television programs, videos, other materials associated with new and emerging technologies or, only through September 2006, news programming;

- Distribute materials through such mechanisms as a loan service; and

- Provide free educational materials, including textbooks, in accessible media for students who are visually impaired and print disabled who are in elementary and secondary schools and in undergraduate and graduate education; to carry out these activities, eligibility is limited to national nonprofit organizations which meet certain criteria specified in the law related to their capacity and track record.

Q
A

What is the new National Instructional Materials Access Center?

Within 1 year of enactment of the amendments the Secretary is required to establish and support the national center through the American Printing House for the Blind. The duties of the center are to:

- Maintain a catalog of print instructional materials made available to the center by textbook publishers and SEAs and LEAs that are prepared in the National Instructional Materials Accessibility Standard. This standard is to be established by the Secretary for use in preparing electronic files suitable and used solely for efficient conversion into specialized formats;

- Provide access to these materials free of charge to blind and other persons with print disabilities in elementary and secondary schools; and

- Develop, adopt, and publish procedures to protect against copyright infringement with respect to print instructional materials supplied to SEAs and LEAs as described in Sec. 612(a)(23) and Sec. 613(a)(6) of the 2004 IDEA Amendments.

How much money was authorized for Subpart 3 activities?

IDEA 2004 authorizes for these activities such sums as may be necessary for each of the fiscal years 2005 through 2010. In making appropriations for the Subpart 3 activities, Congress has appropriated separately for the parent center activities (Parent Training and Information Centers, Community Parent Resource Centers, and the Technical Assistance for the Parent Training and Information Centers) and the technology and media services activities. For FY 2005, Congress appropriated $26.0 million for the parent center activities and $25.7 million for FY 2006 and again for FY 2007. For the technology and media services activities authorized under this subpart, Congress appropriated $38.8 million for FY 2005 and $38.4 million for FY 2006 and again for FY 2007.

GENERAL PROVISIONS

What is the purpose of the General Provisions subpart?

This subpart sets forth requirements and conditions that will apply to grants, cooperative agreements, and contracts awarded under Subparts 2 and 3 of Part D. Several changes were made in the general provisions, including some minor and technical revisions as well as the elimination of some provisions that were in previous law. No significant additions were made by IDEA 2004.

COMPREHENSIVE PLAN FOR SUBPARTS 2 AND 3

What are the overall changes to the Comprehensive Plan?

Since 1997, IDEA has required that the Department develop a comprehensive plan for activities carried out under most Part D programs in order to enhance the provision of early intervention, educational, related, and transitional services to children with disabilities under Parts B and C of the Act. IDEA 2004 continues to require the development of a comprehensive plan, limiting its scope to activities conducted under Subparts 2 and 3 of Part D.

Q

Have changes been made that will affect the development and reporting of the Comprehensive Plan?

A

Yes, Congress authorized several changes. First, although the law continues to require that the Secretary obtain input from the field in developing the plan, it now requires that such input be obtained from interested individuals with relevant expertise rather than specifying, as in previous law, a list of the types of individuals to be consulted in plan development. Thus, the law no longer specifically requires consultation with parents of children with disabilities, nor with representatives of such entities as SEAs, LEAs, higher education, or the National Council on Disability. Second, the Secretary is to coordinate the development of the Comprehensive Plan, to the extent practicable, with the research plan that will be developed and carried out by the National Center for Special Education Research. Third, the Secretary will now be required to provide at least 45 days for public comment on the Comprehensive Plan.

Finally, IDEA 2004 requires that the Secretary report to Congress annually (rather than periodically as under previous law) on activities conducted under Subparts 2 and 3 of Part D. The first report is due 1 year after enactment of the 2004 Amendments, which would be in December 2005.

Q

Will the Comprehensive Plan address research and related activities carried out by IES through its new National Center for Special Education research?

A

Because the research program that was previously authorized under IDEA has been moved to a different law (the Education Sciences Reform Act) and will be administered by a different office in the U.S. Department of Education (the Institute of Education Sciences), the Part D Comprehensive Plan will not address research in the education of children with disabilities as it did under previous law. Instead, this research will be addressed in a plan to be developed by IES and its new National Center for Special Education Research. However, IDEA and ESRA both require that OSEP and IES coordinate the development of their respective plans.

Q

Since IDEA 1997 was enacted, the Office of Special Education Programs has not published proposed priorities for grant funding nor has it solicited public review and comment in advance of publishing its final funding priorities. Will this continue?

A

Yes, this practice is expected to continue under IDEA 2004. IDEA 2004, like IDEA 1997, permits the Secretary generally to bypass governmentwide rules requiring that federal agencies provide the opportunity for public review of, and comment on, proposed grant funding priorities before setting final funding priorities. As long as OSEP develops funding priorities that are consistent with any of several broad topic areas listed in the law, the governmentwide rules can be waived.

Q *Does IDEA continue to require the Secretary to assist historically Black colleges and universities and institutions with significant minority enrollments to participate in Part D activities and to improve outcomes for children with disabilities?*

A Yes, this support is still required under IDEA. Under previous law, at least 1% of most Part D funds were to be set aside to provide technical assistance and outreach activities to historically Black institutions and to institutions with minority enrollments of not less than 25%. IDEA 2004 increases the set-aside to not less than 2% of funds appropriated for Subparts 2 and 3. Although the percentage associated with this set-aside has doubled, it will be computed on a base that no longer includes funds to carry out research activities in the education of children with disabilities. Formerly an IDEA activity, the research program will now be funded through and carried out by another U.S. Department of Education agency, the IES.

Q *IDEA used to permit the Secretary to spend some funds appropriated for one type of Part D activity on other activities authorized under Part D. Is this still the case?*

A No, the statute deleted from the law the provision that provided a certain degree of flexibility to Department officials in the expenditure of funds appropriated under Part D. Under previous law, the Secretary was permitted to use up to 20% of funds appropriated under Part D to carry out any activity as long as such activity was already authorized by, and was consistent with, the purposes of Part D. Current law now requires that funds appropriated for personnel preparation activities, for example, must be spent on activities authorized under that program. Existing Department administrative regulations may permit limited blending of funds across Part D programs but subject to criteria that apply to all Department programs.

Q *What priorities were given to children with gifts and talents under the new IDEA law?*

A In making grants under Part D Personnel Preparation, Technical Assistance, Model Demonstration Projects, Dissemination of Information, or Supports to Improve Results for Children With Disabilities, the Secretary may give priority to awarding grants to projects that address the needs of children with gifts and talents.

ADMINISTRATIVE PROVISIONS

Q *What is the overall purpose of the Administrative Provisions?*

A This section establishes requirements that apply to the U.S. Department of Education as well as to grantees and contractors in the submission and evaluation of applications for funding under Subparts 2 and 3 of Part D and in carrying out funded activities.

Q *For a number of years, IDEA guaranteed minimum levels of Part D funding to address needs in several areas (e.g., deaf-blindness, deafness, and serious emotional disturbance). Are these funding levels still guaranteed?*

A No, the statute deletes the minimum funding levels that have been in IDEA for over a decade. The minimum funding provision was added to the law with the 1997 IDEA amendments at the same time that Congress consolidated what had been approximately 14 discrete discretionary programs into 5 programs to ensure that the needs of certain populations of children with disabilities would continue to receive adequate federal support. As Part D funding and allocations to address the needs of these special populations have increased over time, these minimum funding levels were considered to be unnecessary.

Q *Have any changes been made in the requirements for Standing Panels that review and evaluate applications for funding?*

A Yes, several changes have been made:

- When the Secretary includes parents of children with disabilities as members of peer review panels to evaluate proposals for funding, they must be parents of children with disabilities ages birth through 26.

- IDEA no longer requires the Secretary to provide training to people who are selected to serve as members of Standing Panels.

- Individuals who serve as members of Standing Panels may do so for no more than 3 consecutive years.

Have any changes been made that affect the Department of Education's administration of Part D-funded projects?

Yes, IDEA 2004 deleted two provisions that were in previous law. As a result:

- The Secretary is no longer authorized to use funds appropriated for activities that would be supported under Subparts 2 and 3 of Part D to pay the expenses of federal employees to conduct onsite monitoring of projects that receive more than $500,000 or more a year; and

- The Secretary is no longer authorized to use funds appropriated for Subparts 2 and 3; and

- To evaluate activities supported under those subparts.

EDUCATION SCIENCES REFORM ACT: NATIONAL CENTER FOR SPECIAL EDUCATION RESEARCH

What are the overall changes to the research program in special education?

Under a statutory authority that predates the enactment in 1975 of the IDEA by more than a decade, the federal government has sponsored research and development activities related to the education of children with disabilities. This program of research, designed to improve developmental and educational outcomes for children with disabilities, has been a critical component of the infrastructure of federal assistance provided by IDEA Part D to support State and local efforts to provide a FAPE to children with disabilities. Through IDEA 2004, Congress made significant changes in this program, including removing the research authority from IDEA and moving the administration of the program from the OSEP. A summary of these changes follow.

What administrative changes have been made in the federal program of research to improve results for children with disabilities?

In an effort to consolidate all U.S. Department of Education sponsored research under one unit, Congress moved the responsibility for administering the research program in special education from the OSEP to a new National Center for Special Education Research housed in the Department's research arm, IES. The Institute will be in charge of all U.S. Department of Education research activities, the compilation and analysis of education statistics, and the evaluation of federal programs authorized under the ESEA, IDEA, the Higher Education Act, and other federal education programs.

Q

If IDEA no longer authorizes research in the education of children with disabilities, where does this authority come from?

A

Given the change in how the program would be administered, rather than leave language in IDEA authorizing research activities in the education of children with disabilities, Congress deleted the research provisions in IDEA and added a new research authority in special education to the Education Sciences Reform Act (ESRA). The ESRA, enacted in 2002, is the law that authorizes the research and evaluation activities that are carried out by the Institute of Education Sciences.

Q

When will be these changes go into effect?

A

The transition of the research program in the education of children with disabilities from OSEP to IES took place over the first half of 2005 and was completed by late summer 2006. During that time, the development of the Center's administrative structure and staffing was undertaken, and a commissioner was named. The law requires that the Commissioner have a high level of expertise in the fields of research, research management, and the education of children with disabilities.

Aside from the legal and structural changes, how the nature of the research program will be affected–the priorities it will address, its articulation with the implementation needs of the IDEA state grant programs, the processes and mechanisms it will employ in planning and carrying out its research activities–will emerge over the next few years.

Q

What is the mission of the National Center for Special Education Research?

A

The mission of the center is:

- To sponsor research to expand the knowledge and understanding of the needs of infants, toddlers, and children with disabilities in order to improve their developmental, educational, and transitional results;

- To sponsor research to improve services provided under, and support the implementation of, IDEA; and

- To evaluate the implementation and effectiveness of IDEA, in coordination with the National Center for Education Evaluation and Regional Assistance, another organization within the IES.

Q *Will IES continue to hold Field-Initiated Research, Initial Career Research, and Student-Initiated Research competitions?*

A The answer to this question is not known at this time. All of these competitions fall within the category of "field-initiated" research, which means that within broad parameters set in the statute people in the field are invited to identify issues they believe are in need of research and to propose a plan to the agency for conducting investigations in those areas. In addition to the Field-Initiated Research competition, which has been held for many years, OSEP has also provided opportunities for doctoral students to propose and conduct such studies on a small scale, and for individuals in the early years of their research careers to pursue research support in a separate competition. Both of these mechanisms were designed to foster and support the early development of researchers and their programs of research in special education and related fields.

IES's authorizing legislation requires that it support field-initiated research. However, since its creation in 2002, IES has not conducted such research competitions, favoring instead to invite proposals which address agency-directed research priorities.

Q *Will the new National Center for Special Education Research provide funding for model demonstration and outreach projects?*

A The answer to this question appears to be no. IDEA retains this authority under Sec. 663 (Technical Assistance and Dissemination), and early but unofficial indications from IES suggest that model demonstration and outreach projects will not be part of the agency's research agenda in special education. However, as the new National Center develops its research plan over the next few years, a compelling need to support such projects could be identified. The statutory language that authorizes the new National Center does not prohibit it from including such funding within the scope of its research program.

Q *Will research projects that were awarded before the enactment of the 2004 Amendments be terminated as a result of the changes in the research program?*

A No, IDEA 2004 requires that all such projects will continue in accordance with the terms of their original awards.

Understanding IDEA 2004:
Frequently Asked Questions

Miscellaneous
Title III: Effective Dates

Miscellaneous

Q

A

TITLE III: EFFECTIVE DATES

What are the effective dates of the law?

All portions of IDEA 2004 went into effect on July 1, 2005, except for the following provisions:

- The following provisions went into effect on December 3, 2004:

  - Requirements for highly qualified special education teachers

  - The following sections of Part D:

    - Personnel Preparation

    - Technical Assistance

    - Model Demonstration Projects

    - Dissemination of Information

    - Supports to Improve Results for Children with Disabilities

    - General Provisions

  - The National Center For Special Education Research

- The Special Education Research Commissioner's plan went into effect October 1, 2005.

Council for Exceptional Children

The voice and vision of special education

Understanding IDEA 2004: Frequently Asked Questions

Appendix
Frequently Used Acronyms

Appendix

FREQUENTLY USED ACRONYMS

BIP	behavioral intervention plan
CSPD	Comprehensive system of personnel development
IDEA	Individuals With Disabilities Education Act 1997 and 2004
EIS	early intervening services
ESEA	Elementary and Secondary Education Act of 1965
ESRA	Education Sciences Reform Act of 2002
FAPE	free and appropriate public education
FICC	Federal Interagency Coordinating Council
HOUSSE	high objective uniform state standard of evaluation
IEP	individualized education program
IES	Institute of Education Sciences
IFSP	individualized family services plan
LEA	local education agency
LRE	least restrictive environment
NCLB	No Child Left Behind Act of 2001
NIMAC	National Instructional Materials Accessibility Center
NIMAS	National Instructional Materials Accessibility Standard
OSEP	Office of Special Education Programs
PTIs	Parent Training and Information Centers

SEA   state education agency

SIG   state improvement grant

SLD   specific learning disability

SPP   state performance plan

TA   technical assistance